Your Towns and Cities in

# Ludlow

## in the Great War

# Dedication

This book is dedicated not only to the hundreds of men who died, fighting for their king and country, in the Great War, but also to the men who survived, damaged in many ways, and returned to rebuild their lives. It is also dedicated to the thousands of women who, despite the anguish they endured, rolled up their sleeves to help in the war effort both at home and abroad. The war may have had a very different outcome without them. I would also like to mention the conscientious objectors who fought the war in their own way, with no less determination or courage.

Your Towns and Cities in the Great War

# Ludlow
## in the Great War

Julie Phillips

Pen & Sword
**MILITARY**

First published in Great Britain in 2016 by
PEN & SWORD MILITARY
*an imprint of*
Pen and Sword Books Ltd
47 Church Street
Barnsley
South Yorkshire S70 2AS

Copyright © Julie Phillips, 2016

ISBN 978 1 47382 816 2

The right of Julie Phillips to be identified as the author of
this work has been asserted by her in accordance with the Copyright,
Designs and Patents Act 1988.

A CIP record for this book is available from the British Library

All rights reserved. No part of this book may be reproduced or transmitted
in any form or by any means, electronic or mechanical including
photocopying, recording or by any information storage and retrieval
system, without permission from the Publisher in writing.

Printed and bound in England
by CPI Group (UK) Ltd, Croydon, CR0 4YY

Typeset in Times New Roman by Chic Graphics

*Pen & Sword Books Ltd incorporates the imprints of*
Pen & Sword Archaeology, Atlas, Aviation, Battleground, Discovery,
Family History, History, Maritime, Military, Naval, Politics, Railways,
Select, Social History, Transport, True Crime, Claymore Press,
Frontline Books, Leo Cooper, Praetorian Press, Remember When,
Seaforth Publishing and Wharncliffe.


*For a complete list of Pen and Sword titles please contact*
Pen and Sword Books Limited
47 Church Street, Barnsley, South Yorkshire, S70 2AS, England
E-mail: enquiries@pen-and-sword.co.uk
Website: www.pen-and-sword.co.uk

# Contents

# Acknowledgements

Many thanks to all the following:

Derek Beattie
Julie Brook
Annette Burgoyne
Chris Deaves and all at the
  Ecclesiastic Offices
Margaret Edwards
Harper Adams Agricultural
  University
Jan Johnson
Daniel Lockett
*Ludlow Advertiser*
Ludlow Library
Ludlow Resource Centre
Caroline Magnus
Dorothy Nicole

Christopher Owen
Jean Parker
David Phillips
Isobel Phillips
Margory Sheldon
Shropshire County Library
  Service
*Shropshire Star*
Clifford Smout
Fred Tipton
Simon Whaley
Stanley Williams
The Wellcome Trust
*The Wellington Journal and
Shrewsbury News*

**Abbreviations used:**

**FAU**: Friends' Ambulance Unit
**KSLI**: King's Shropshire Light Infantry
*LA*: *Ludlow Advertiser*
**RAMC**: Royal Army Medical Corps
**VAD**: Voluntary Aid Detachment
*WJ*: *Wellington Journal*

# CHAPTER 1

# A Brief History of Ludlow

Before the First World War Ludlow was, as it very much still is today, a bustling and thriving market town with strong agricultural links. Successful livestock markets were held with animals being bought and sold from across the county and beyond. The town, despite being affluent with its upmarket stores and elegant housing, as with many similar towns in the country had its fair share of poor housing including dilapidated buildings with pockets of poor people needing relief.

The Bull Ring, 1900s. (*Courtesy of Fred Tipton*)

St Laurence's Church tower, 2015. (*Author's own*)

Ludlow Town scene, 1900s. (*Courtesy of Fred Tipton*)

One of the main focal points of the town is St Laurence's Church. Although the church suffered a downturn in success and popularity in the years prior to the war, it was still the cornerstone of many of its parishioners' lives. It offered relief to the poor as well as ministering to the town's spiritual and community needs. St Laurence's Church with its imposing tower can be seen from miles around and on the approach to the town.

On the other side of town St Peter's Roman Catholic Church would soon extend its welcome to the Belgian refugees, the majority of whom were Catholics. The ruins of a once spectacular castle were also often the centrepiece of many a community or civic gathering as they are today. It is easy to see why those early settlers in the area decided to

The Market Square, Ludlow, 1900s. (*Courtesy of Fred Tipton*)

Lower Broad Street, Ludlow, 1900s. (*Courtesy of Fred Tipton*)

base themselves there with its strong vantage point, nestled along the borders between Shropshire and Wales. The River Teme that runs through the town provided power for water mills and also splendid fishing. It is these and many other of its majestic landmarks that make Ludlow easily recognizable on approach.

Ludlow's origins stretch as far back as 1086 when it is thought the imposing castle first built by the de Lacy family was a strategically-placed fortress to keep the Welsh at bay. Typically of the medieval grid pattern, longer, broader streets are interlaced with narrower lanes that lead to the market place. To defend the town, its walls were built in 1233; these originally had seven gates, the sites of which can still all be seen today.

It was a fortified town, capable of defending itself from invading armies and keeping villains and criminals out, although the townsfolk didn't want to deter people from spending their money and trading there. The market place was, therefore, also important; not solely for

Ludlow Castle, 2015. (*Courtesy of Isobel Phillips*)

The Broad Gate, 2015. (*Courtesy of Isobel Phillips*)

commerce but somewhere that people could also buy essential commodities and as a social meeting place, pretty much as it still is today. With its plethora of shops and market stalls, the long-held traditions are still evident today with the annual Medieval Christmas Fayre, agricultural show and food festival.

Going back to its humble beginnings, in 1377 there were 1,172 tax-paying residents. The town soon expanded and held its markets every week with the growth of its industries following suit, leading to some townsfolk becoming fairly wealthy. It was a prosperous and vibrant town, particularly within the wool, cloth and livestock arenas.

Broad Street, Ludlow, 1900s. (*Courtesy of Fred Tipton*)

Ludlow today as seen from the Whitcliffe. (*Author's own*)

It wasn't, however, until King Edward IV decided in 1472 to base the headquarters of the Council of the Marches in the town that Ludlow truly began to grow and gain in reputation and power.

Wandering through the streets of Ludlow, it is easy to see how the town expanded through the centuries, as nestling next to medieval buildings are those of a more recent grand Georgian appearance. In the eighteenth and nineteenth centuries the town was an important meeting-place for socialites with glove-making the town's top industry and the railway arriving in the town, linking it to Shrewsbury and Hereford, a boon for its market place.

Market Square, Ludlow, 2015. (*Courtesy of Isobel Phillips*)

The town has a wonderful array of medieval buildings, including some beautiful architecture, and was renowned for its numerous inns, many of which are still in operation today.

However, for around thirty years prior to the beginning of the First World War, the town experienced an economic downturn, as did many

An example of Ludlow's beautiful architecture, 2015. (*Author's own*)

The Feather's Inn, Ludlow; one of the oldest inns in the town. (*Courtesy of Isobel Phillips*)

similar towns across the country. There were many reasons for this, not least the decline in agriculture and the fact that other towns could obtain coal and cloth more easily and cheaply and the population growth had plateaued.

The Buttermarket, Ludlow, 2015. (*Courtesy of Isobel Phillips*)

The local community certainly enjoyed their entertainment with regular fêtes and fayres and an annual agricultural and horticultural show, unsurprising for a rural area. Ludlow had a successful cricket team and bowls team who regularly played matches and football was also a regular feature. While the threat of war was upon them, they still made good use of the local sporting fields; this was not at all a popular decision in some residents' opinions.

The town also fared well in educating its young. There was a distinguished and well-thought-of grammar school offering top-class education to the upper classes. They would also, in the coming years, see many of their old boys engage in the war effort, many of them giving their lives. There were also national schools and a workhouse. Charity was an important part of community life, with the rich only too happy to contribute.

Nationally, Great Britain was an affluent country that had built up a wide empire. India and parts of Africa and Australia, among others, were colonies and Britain was building its wealth with their help. Little did the townspeople know that in a few years' time they would find themselves in the middle of a bloody war that raged across the world and put their community and livelihoods to the test. The castle, the town's stronghold, had seen them through many a trying time and just as the castle had stood the testament of time, could the townspeople show their mettle in the traumatic times of war and come out of it, not unscathed but salvageable?

A cannon outside the castle; defence was never far from the minds of Ludlow's inhabitants. (*Courtesy of Isobel Phillips*)

# CHAPTER 2

# War Breaks Out

*'The Lights Are Going Out All Over Europe ...'*

**Assassination**

Considering the potential disaster that the events leading up to Great Britain's entry into the war were about to cause, the local newspapers made very little fuss about the assassination of Archduke Franz Ferdinand on 28 June 1914 by a Serbian Gavrilo Princip. In fact, the small article about this was placed above an advert for Bird's Custard!

When war was formally declared on 4 August 1914, no one in Ludlow expected it, let alone predicted that it would turn into the most violent and long-winded, bloody battle that the world had ever known. (This followed the preliminary invasion of Serbia by Austria-Hungary, and Russian support of Serbia.) Germany then declared war on Russia, involving subsequent plans to invade France, but even then there was barely a nod in the local newspapers to indicate that Great Britain, including her sons in Ludlow and the whole community, was about to be thrown into turmoil for four years that would cost them dearly in so many unimaginable ways. There had, of course, been trouble brewing, particularly in the Balkans and, closer to home, the issue of Home Rule in Ireland. If anything was about to kick off, it would be here, surely?

**The Best-laid Plans**

While life carried on at home, the Schlieffen Plan was beginning to be put into force abroad. The idea was for German armed forces to advance to the west through Belgium and Northern France while other flanks closed in and Paris would be encircled. The plan was supposed to take no more than forty days, which is why it was thought that the whole event would be over by Christmas 1914. In fact, only a few days before the outbreak of war, there were reports in the *Ludlow Advertiser* of fighting in Dublin at Howarth Harbour and it was this trouble that was uppermost in people's minds around this time.

When the people of Ludlow read that 'extreme activities' were taking place in the dockyards of Great Britain 'in making preparation against any untoward result of the European situation' and that leave was on the whole being stopped, they, as indeed in many other cities, towns and villages across Great Britain, might just have begun to think that war was not as far away from their rural farms and front doors as they had hoped.

Despite the threats faced by the British people, the order of the day was very much to stand up for their convictions, honour, values and integrity and this would stand the Empire, Great Britain and towns such as Ludlow in good stead through the coming years. The realization soon came that Britain was at war and the British public would have no option but to support it.

**The Government takes Control**
As news of the war sank in, the government passed several new laws such as making provision for men who would be wounded in the war and their dependants, registering aliens and controlling the 'too many' Germans living in Great Britain, increasing the amount of coins, providing paper money and making postal orders legal tender. Measures were also being put in place for the regulation of retail prices and groceries to prevent extortionate price hikes.

When news reports came in from other parts of the country that some 'needlessly alarmed' customers were making 'excessive purchases', they were vilified and the British public was warned that their 'unreasonable conduct cannot be too strongly deprecated'. Within government ranks, the rousing speeches and rattling of swords were designed to give the British public confidence and boost their patriotism in the face of the adversity that was now approaching.

'In its hour of trial and danger the country has the supreme advantage of unity,' said Mr Bonar Law. He was the one-time

Conservative MP for Glasgow Blackfriars in 1900 and then Parliamentary Secretary to the Board of Trade in 1902. A plain yet charismatic speaker, he earned respect and became Leader of the Conservative Party in 1911 but conceded to Lloyd George's premiership, playing a key role in his new War Cabinet. A unified Great Britain fighting against a common enemy was what the British military and government wanted to show the German aggressors.

The railways were now controlled by the state, being used, in part, for the transportation of troops. The state would also be controlling the distribution of food supplies. Even the August bank holiday was extended by three days to prevent panic-buying and a run on the banks.

It had been hoped that this initial 'little tiff' between Serbia and Austria-Hungary would stay just that. They were merely flexing their muscles and the gnashing of teeth would remain between them, wouldn't it? However, the rumour and propaganda machine was in overdrive, leading to a hotbed of mistrust, inflamed anger, posturing and power-plays, fuelled by misunderstandings and miscomprehensions about each country involved regarding exactly what they were up to.

Germany wanted more than it had at the time and was prepared to fight for it. Thank goodness we were out of it. However, Germany then threatened a little country called Belgium and, due to a treaty signed by the British in 1829 promising to come to Belgium's aid should they ever be invaded and their neutrality threatened, we were suddenly drawn into the affray.

Germany was chomping at the bit and grabbed an opportunity which they exploited by declaring war. Russia, Britain and France were in no fit state to get out of the war and they certainly were not co-ordinated or organized to run into a fully-fledged battle, either in a military sense or politically.

The Home Rule issue in Ireland was immediately put on hold. It was every Irishman's duty to come to the aid of their fellow countrymen and fight for their lives and they did their country proud until the Easter Uprisings of 1916 when, despite the raging war in which the world was engaged, there was an outbreak of rioting and violence.

Back in Ludlow, the townspeople were shocked that war had been declared. Little did they know, when the news broke, just how much the war was going to change their lives, forever. While the rest of

Britain was girding its loins and getting troops, supplies and plans in order, the town of Ludlow was also preparing itself.

### Flytraps and Soufflé

It was within the pages of the *LA* that we first get wind that things were afoot in the town when it featured an appeal by the Duke of Portland from Welbeck Abbey. He was speaking at the Agricultural Society luncheon for tenants and said: 'It is the bounden duty of every one of us to put aside personal opinions, personal prejudices, and personal conveniences. It behoves all of us to keep brave hearts, and that which is most likely to ensue from that keeping of brave hearts – cool heads.'

Indeed, the *Advertiser* itself had a few ideas on how best the town could react to news of the war. 'Keep Calm and Carry On' seemed to be the message! They advised readers against too much excitement and to think about the impact of their actions on others. The hoarding of supplies, particularly food and gold, was frowned upon and deemed horribly unpatriotic. People were reminded that there was always someone worse off than themselves. Employers in the town were asked not to shut down or lay off their workers but to reduce hours instead. However, one of the most important things the ordinary folk of Ludlow could do would be to support, cheer and encourage their soldiers, while also taking time to help those who did not understand war what it was all about.

If, however, you read the 'Ladies Home Column' in the same issue you wouldn't be able to help thinking that the ladies of Ludlow were more interested in making war against the housefly than Germany! The main items in this column concerned making flytraps and lemon soufflé.

The Earl of Plymouth (best known as Clive of India), who had a stately home in the area, supported the war and in an address at St Fagan's Castle, his seat in Glamorgan, he urged the country to unite and fight as one, setting their political and ideological differences aside.

The outbreak of war immediately affected the council too, with the Mayor of Ludlow informing the council that one of their members, the surveyor Captain Lane, would be going to war. In addition, the matter of the Cemetery Board's attempts to get the council to adopt the local government bye-laws was deemed to be unimportant now that there was a war on.

Hopes were still high in the town that war would be avoided but there were 'ominous' signs that this would not be so, particularly the announcement by the railway company that had been commissioned to take the Ludlow Wesleyan Sunday School children on their trips to Llandudno and Blackpool that these would now not take place.

**The Announcement**

On 4 August 1914 the town crier strode through the streets of Ludlow proclaiming that the mayor Councillor Valentine would give further information about the war and how it would affect them as a town at the Town Hall at 11am.

The day was a local holiday and as many trips out had been abandoned, there were many more townspeople at home than there would normally have been. As the crowds gathered outside the Town

Note the soldiers in the front rows listening to the declaration of war, 1914. (*Courtesy of Shropshire County Museum Service*)

Crowd listening to the declaration of war, 1914. (*Courtesy of Shropshire County Museum Service*)

Hall, Captain Lane and Lieutenant Marston along with G Company of the Territorials stood, waiting. There was a platform that housed the Standard of Scotland, England and Wales. It was estimated that there were some 200 to 300 people waiting to hear what the mayor had to say that day. There was a cheer from the crowd as Captain Lane carried the Union Jack to the platform.

An anxious quiet fell upon the crowd as the mayor read out the king's declaration: the Royal Navy Reserve Officers were to be called for active duty, along with the men of the Royal Navy Reserve, Royal Fleet Reserve and the Royal Naval Volunteer Reserve, extended time of service for expired men in the navy to five years; permission was granted for the requisition of any British ship or vessel, and the payment of some bills of exchange. Three cheers for the king sounded around the town and the National Anthem was sung.

This was not to be the only such gathering. The following Wednesday a further five proclamations were read by the mayor that included soldiers' continuing service in the army would be for as long as needed; the Defence of the Realm Act (DORA) came into force; the Army Reserves and the Territorial forces were called out; exports were stopped; and there would be an extended bank holiday.

**Your Country Needs You**
The British army in peacetime was relatively small at around 750,000 men and it is well-documented that there was difficulty with enlistment. The media at the time did link this apathy to the Kaiser's plans for invasion as he knew the British army was so small. When it is considered that the German army comprised around 4,000,000 men, it's no wonder the Kaiser was laughing. However, when his plans became apparent and Belgium was invaded, Great Britain and the Empire were given a rude awakening and the men were galvanized into action.

In a regular section of the local newspaper, 'Local War Items', it was claimed it was possible that Shropshire was leading the way in its recruitment of men. It was estimated that in the first few weeks of the war the King's Shropshire Light Infantry (KSLI) had 1,200 men; the Shropshire Yeomanry 1,400 men; the Shropshire Royal Horse Artillery 220 men; the RAMC 250 men; Shropshire men belonging to other units 500; and Lord Kitchener's New Army a further 300 men; giving a grand total of 3,870 Shropshire men. Nationally, by the middle of

Ludlow Troop of the Shropshire Yeomanry. (*Courtesy of Shropshire County Museum Service*)

August 1914 Germany had 1,077 battalions in the field, while the British had only forty-eight. Drastic measures to recruit men were required.

One of the new Acts to be legislated during the war was DORA. This Act, among other things, gave the power to the authorities to stop people attempting to communicate with the enemy, especially the giving or receiving of sensitive information that could jeopardize operations of the armed forces. There was also special provision for the protection of means of communication: railways, docks, telegraph poles, the Post Office and harbours, for example. More conditions would be added to DORA as the war progressed, including the rule that employers in ship-building, engineering, the production of arms, ammunition or explosives could only employ those who lived within a 10-mile radius of the place of work.

Other national changes were the introduction of new bank notes by the then Chancellor Lloyd George to replace the older £1 and £10 notes in an attempt to stop forgeries. An emergency Bill was also put together, the results of which are still felt today with the restriction of the sale of alcohol and amendments to DORA.

Up until the end of August 1914, the Shropshire Territorial Volunteers totalled 623 members of the 4th Battalion, KSLI. The Shropshire Lads, including those from Ludlow and the surrounding area, certainly did their towns and villages, their county, and their king and country proud. However, there were concerns that the enlistment rate, for a town of Ludlow's size, was pitiful.

The main military depot for the county was in Shrewsbury and was regarded as one of the most important military organizations in the country. It formed the headquarters for four districts: Wales, Cheshire, Shropshire, Herefordshire and Monmouthshire, as well as being the headquarters for the Welsh Territorial Division, Shropshire Light Infantry, Cheshire Regiment, Royal Welsh Fusiliers, South Wales Borderers, the Welsh Regiment and the South Lancashire Regiment.

As soon as war broke out, it was already known that Shrewsbury Barracks would be playing a key role in the war effort. The order to mobilize was given at Shrewsbury on the Tuesday at 5pm and they were more than ready with posters and orders posted on all public buildings and places of worship.

## Conscription
As more soldiers and sailors fell on the battlefields and at sea, the government knew that they were running out of men. Fewer volunteers

The Ludlow Volunteers. (*Courtesy of Shropshire County Museum Service*)

came forward, partially, no doubt, through fear and not wanting to become another statistic. These men were seen by many as cowards and shirkers for failing to do their duty for king and country. They, alongside men who had previously been exempt from active duty, would soon find themselves being hunted down or their appeals and exemptions being turned down at the local tribunals. Conscription, under the Derby Scheme, was to be introduced in 1916.

Conscription was deemed a necessary evil as there were 651,160 unstarred single men who had not enlisted. (Some occupations and employees of certain industries were exempt from being called up and these men were starred.) The former were being blamed for the situation in which the country now found itself. If they weren't prepared to fight voluntarily, then they would have to be forced to do so.

It seems, though, that the government and those facing conscription couldn't do anything right in the eyes of certain quarters. A cartoon, titled 'Recruiting for the Imp Army', featured in the local press on 8 January showed various imps in uniform with captions such as 'Just the fellow for Black Watch', 'I'll be all right at taking cover' and under a section of the cartoon showing two imps wearing signs reading 'totally deaf and blind'. The cartoon was poking fun at the fact that it appeared they'd take anyone into the army now whether they were up to the job or not because they were so desperate for men.

The Military Service Bill stated that all British males (except Irish) between the ages of 18 and 41, unmarried or widowers without dependants, would have to enlist. The only exceptions would be those not usually resident in Great Britain, members of the forces (Reserve or Territorial) when liable for Foreign Service, men in the navy, Royal Marines, or those recommended for exemption, the Admiralty, or men of the church.

Exemptions would be those with dependants who would not be able to care for themselves if the main breadwinner went to war, workers whose jobs were of national importance, those incapable of fighting due to ill health or injury, and conscientious objectors. As a footnote, however, conscientious objectors would be encouraged to serve in non-combatant roles. Conscription was not welcomed by many sectors of society who saw it as a strike against freedom and democracy. However, if the war was to be won, men had to be found from somewhere to fight it.

# CHAPTER 3

# The Call to Arms

*'The world's at war, I want to go. The trumpet's call rings clear.'*

**It will all be over by Christmas**

At the beginning of the war there was a common notion that 'it will all be over by Christmas'; however, which Christmas that might be was another matter. Initially, when war was announced, it was the British Expeditionary Force (BEF) that saw action first. Then the reservists, Territorials, KSLI and Shropshire Yeomanry were called back to active service.

Before the war Great Britain effectively had two armies: the part-time Territorial Forces and the regular army (the latter was referred to as the BEF when sent to France on service in both world wars.) However, it soon became clear that this would not be enough and Lord Kitchener's well-known 'Your Country Needs You' campaign was launched. Its mission was to find and train 100,000 volunteers to form his 'New Army'. Initially the response was generally deemed to be good in Shropshire, although not everyone was happy about the low numbers enlisting in Ludlow. Recruitment drives, including a National Recruitment Day on 2 October 1915 when a rally was held during inclement weather in Castle Square, were put in place but did not have the desired effect.

In September 1914, forty men had signed up to Kitchener's New Army and marched along Corve Street where the recruiting office was situated. The town band played and led them to the station where they

8 Corve Street, Ludlow; the location of the recruiting office, 2015. (*Author's own*)

left for their headquarters. By October of the same year only fifty-two men had volunteered to join the New Army. The total number of recruits from the town and surrounding villages that were enrolled by Mr J.E. Marston and Colour Sergeant J. Flattery was 173.

**Farmers' Sons Hear the Call**

The *WJ* at the time reported on the spectacular scenes of the Shropshire Yeomanry and the Territorials in Ludlow at their headquarters: 'It was a splendid sight to see the smart lot of farmers' sons coming along the streets in numbers of 9 and 10 with their excellent horses. Such a scene as has never been witnessed in Ludlow before.'

The men were to be billeted in the town's inns and hotels overnight with the Territorials having been given orders to carry on to Barry Docks in Wales. It must have been a wonderful sight for the townspeople who arrived in their hundreds to watch their menfolk depart. Of the 110 expected, there were only three men missing at the time.

Not all the men who attended were allowed to join their comrades as they failed the medical, being turned away for reasons such as a dislocated wrist, heart problems, lung disease or other ailments. Men were very badly needed but the officials still had to adhere to their guidelines. The military wanted men who could stand up to the rigours of battle, and weak or ill men would just be a liability.

While the men were waiting to depart they were confined to base under martial law, receiving rations such as corned beef, bread and coffee for dinner. There were reports of the singing of popular songs,

KSLI, Ludlow, 1915. (*Courtesy of Shropshire County Museum Service*)

KSLI at Barry, South Wales, 1915. (*Courtesy of Shropshire County Museum Service*)

accompanied by a 'Tommy' on the piano. The singing was described as being of the standard only a 'band of comrades' could produce.

On the day of their departure the station and route were lined with spectators who also crammed themselves above the railway bridge and platforms, the officials struggling to contain them. The crowd, estimated to total 4,000 in number, spilled out over the embankment into adjacent fields. The scene was likened to a football cup final. It was a chance for the town to show their gratitude to those of their men that were off to fight and show the Kaiser 'what for'. It was also a chance to say goodbye, for no one knew when or even if they would see their loved ones again. The company then marched to the station with the townspeople applauding and cheering, sending them away as heroes.

The troop train arrived at 8.55pm and as it began to move off a 'terrific roar' sounded from the crowd and didn't stop until the train was out of sight. The women of the town waved their handkerchiefs and squealed with excitement, while the men waved their hats and sticks. A cheer could be heard in response from the troops on the train.

Once again the mayor had been on hand to give a speech. He lauded the townspeople for turning out and the men who had reacted so promptly to the call to arms. He was certain that every one of them would do their duty when faced with the enemy and the whole town would want them home safe, sound and swiftly.

The railway station was again busy on that first Wednesday afternoon after war had been declared, heralding a busy scene with many army reservists boarding trains for the depot at Shrewsbury.

Private Alfred Morris departing on a train in Canada (leaning out on the right, holding a cap). (*Courtesy of Shropshire County Museum Service*)

Many women and children from Ludlow turned up to see the spectacle. Some of them were said to have been crying, particularly those 'who have already known the horrors of war … could not refrain from showing their grief.'

Ludlow also had its very own Volunteer Training Corps, a national initiative, to help defend Great Britain against invasion. They were not provided with any weaponry and their ranks contained men not eligible for enlistment. By November 1914 there were ninety-eight volunteers with training taking place under the watchful eye of John Flattery at the Drill Hall.

Private Alfred Morris and his friend Bert Eaton. (*Courtesy of Shropshire County Museum Service*)

**The Race to the Front**

Once war had been declared things moved swiftly, with the Shropshire Yeomanry also being mobilized. The Ludlow Squadron was called back to duty under the command of Major J.P. Heywood-Lorsdale. C Squadron of the Shropshire Territorial Yeomanry was soon hot on the heels of the Kaiser when they assembled at the Drill Hall, having been billeted in the town. There was a daily inspection of the men and the horses while they awaited further orders. The 4th Shropshire Territorials (Light Infantry) were in Aberystwyth at the time they were ordered to mobilize, so they travelled back to Ludlow and Wellington. Ludlow was ready and waiting.

Ludlow, due to its geographical position near the borders of Wales and Herefordshire, provided the gateway for regiments from across those borders to access Shrewsbury and beyond and so was a hotbed of activity as more and more troops were called to active duty and travelled to their training grounds and thence to the battlefields.

There was also great excitement when, in the week of 15 August 1914, the streets of Ludlow, most notably Old Street and the Bull Ring, were a mass of people due to a large transport section passing through. What a spectacle the sight of forty under-lieutenants and sixty horses from the 3rd Monmouthshire Regiment of the Welsh Border Infantry Brigade must have been. There were also fourteen wagons, many of which bore the names of the farmers and businesses from whom they had been commandeered. The men were also billeted in the town overnight.

This wasn't the last transport section to come through the town either. In the same week over a dozen wagons and armed rearguard hurtled through the town without stopping, having come up from Herefordshire. Even the Shropshire Boy Scouts were called to duty by Lord Harlech, Commissioner of the Scouts. He had received a telegram from the Chief Scout Sir Robert Baden-Powell, hoping for 1,000 scouts to be prepared to help the war effort locally. Such duties could include communications and distribution of information, guarding culverts, helping the Post Office and guarding sections of the Birmingham Aqueduct, etc.

However, it wasn't just men that were needed. Horses were a highly sought-after commodity too. With Ludlow being agriculturally based, with the Ludlow Hunters and the strong, heavy farm horses, they were in good supply and in good condition, something that did not pass unnoticed by the military.

The military men responsible for the acquisition of horses came to Ludlow from Shrewsbury on several occasions. One such visit occurred on Saturday of the week of 15 August 1914 when seventeen horses were taken away by train. Nothing got past these men, as one poor milkman on his early-morning round found out. The men stopped him and enquired how far he had to go before he finished his round. When they discovered it was only a mile or so down the road, they took the horse from him and he continued on foot.

Some of those who chose not to fight did so for what seemed to them to be good reasons. Some were married with children and were afraid they would be leaving their families in hardship should they not come back, despite reassurances from the government that their dependants would be well cared for. Others were concerned that their old job would not be there when they returned. For some, they were simply too old, ill or they were disabled and unfit to fight. For others, it was more of a theological concern.

**Conscientious Objectors and Pacifists**
Conscientious objectors and pacifists were men who did not want to go to war to fight due to their religious or ideological beliefs. One such religious group was the Quakers whose Peace Declaration of 1661 urged them to renounce any violence or war. So when conscription came into force in 1916, many of them signed the register as conscientious objectors, meaning that they would not go and fight for their country. This did not, however, exclude them from doing their patriotic duty in other, non-combatant ways. Unfortunately, there was also room for laziness or defiance as shown by this statement in the local paper:

> The man who honestly and as a matter of conscience objects to combatant service is entitled to exemption. While care must be taken that the man who shirks his duty to his country does not find unworthy shelter behind the provision, every consideration should be given to the man whose objection genuinely rests on religious or moral convictions.

Suddenly finding God or a new moral stance would not suffice. In fact, all men who registered as conscientious objectors faced an interview at a tribunal and there were three options from which to choose: join the armed forces in a non-combatant role (for example, in the RAMC), take on another role in the civilian service, or be exempt from any of the above.

However, just because a man had certain moral convictions or religious beliefs it did not automatically mean he would be granted exemption. It had to be proved. Many conscientious objectors found themselves in prison under extremely difficult and harsh conditions such as hard labour.

Meanwhile, the Quakers didn't just rest on their laurels. It was they who set up the Friends' Ambulance Unit in 1914 and the Friends' Relief Service; these were regarded by them as alternatives to going into service in more conventional combatant roles. However, even this caused problems among the Quakers themselves when those in the FAU agreed to work alongside the military authorities on the front lines. The FAU ceased to exist by 1919 but more than 1,000 people had worked within it across Italy, France, Germany, Great Britain and Belgium during the First World War. After the war, in the early 1920s the Quakers responded to the lack of food by starting up a feeding programme that would come to the aid of around 5 million children.

**Ramping up the Recruitment Drive**
The recruitment drive was very much dependent on the men being aware of what was expected of them and that enlistment and volunteering to fight for their king and country was the right thing to do. Propaganda was a useful tool employed by the government and the military as a way of ensuring that men would be queuing up to enlist. Reports of 'German Atrocities' blazed across the headlines of the newspapers on a regular basis.

There were similar reports of Germans killing babies and women. Undoubtedly there were acts of barbarism that occurred on all sides and probably the German papers were full of similar stories about the French, Belgian and British soldiers too; however, in time of war it is often difficult to separate fact from propaganda.

To show appreciation to those men who had answered the call, an advert was placed by local picture-frame manufacturer A.W. Packer at 147 Corve Street in the *LA* in December 1916 for war shrines. These were memorials, often makeshift, sited away from churches, in the streets, windows, etc. They became very popular up and down the country. There was also going to be a public roll of honour for which the design and estimates were in motion.

Because the military were rapidly running out of men despite reservists being recalled, volunteers and campaigns such as Lord Kitchener's, they soon had to resort to conscription in the form of national service. This was not a popular decision in some quarters but a welcome development in others. There was nowhere left for the 'shirkers' to hide. If they wouldn't volunteer to fight, then they would jolly well be forced to do so.

The classification of men according to occupation, health, etc., was changed several times during the course of the war in a bid to boost numbers. The men were also subjected to a variety of tests to ascertain their fitness to fight. Of course, some men who were keen to avoid fighting would try to fake illness or exaggerate any mild ailment or injury. For example, men in Class A were expected to be able to march, have sufficiently good eyesight to shoot, have good hearing and be able to withstand active service in the trenches. Men of Class B (B1) were to be free of disease, able to march 5 miles, able to see to shoot with glasses and have good hearing, whereas Class B (B2) men could walk to and from work and see and hear well enough for normal activities.

By 1918 the situation was getting desperate. The problem was clear: they needed more men and they needed them now. The new Military Service Bill saw the upper age limit of those eligible to fight raised to 50 and, in certain cases, to 55. All men employed in agriculture of Grade 1 or Class A and not medically graded or classified who were born between and including 1895 to 1899 would be required to enlist with all their previous exemptions cancelled.

Whether they volunteered, were in the regular army or were conscripted, the men of Ludlow did their best on the battlefields and seas of the Great War. With the situation and subsequent directives changing hour by hour, it was not an easy job keeping abreast of who was sent where and for how long. Communications were not always accurate and often took several days to reach their destination, by which time the situation would quite likely have changed again. This made things very difficult for the families left behind, who must have wondered whether or not their loved ones were safe.

# CHAPTER 4

# Who Fought?

**Fighting for King and Country**

We have already heard about the KSLI and the Yeomanry's preparations for joining the war offensive, but who were the individual faces that made up the numbers? In the appalling casualty figures from the Great War it is easy to forget that each one of these was someone's son, husband or brother. Looking at the names on the war memorials now and listening to their names being read out on Remembrance Day ceremonies across the country, it is hard to imagine these brave souls as the young men who walked the streets of Ludlow, attended its schools and played in its streets. It is impossible within the pages of this book to mention every single name but what follows are some local lads' war experiences.

The first man from Ludlow to lose his life in the conflict was John Henry Baron. The news of his death was a blow to the local community and another soldier, also from Ludlow, Corporal C.A. Francis of the 1st KSLI mentioned it in a letter to his old headmaster Mr J. Diggle of the National Schools, published in the *LA* of 7 November 1914: '… I am pleased to tell you up to the present only one Ludlow boy has been killed. The old boy who was killed died a quick, merciful death. He was shot through the head and died almost instantly.'

Mr Diggle, as well as receiving many letters from his previous pupils now engaged in war, was to become no stranger to personal tragedy when his son H. Victor Diggle was killed in 1918. Lance Corporal Hubert Victor Diggle lived with his mother Esther and father John in Julian Road, Ludlow. While he attended Ludlow Grammar

School he engaged in drama, having played Marley's ghost in a school production in 1912. He was also a gifted sportsman, playing soccer a year later. Hubert was in the 10th (Shropshire and Cheshire Yeomanry) KSLI and is buried in France.

## All at Sea

Another man born in Ludlow, Midshipman Charles Raynsford Longley, died aged just 18 when his ship HMS *Indefatigable* was sunk in the Battle of Jutland on 31 May 1916. He came from a military family, his father being Major General Sir John R. Longley who commanded the 1st Battalion, East Surreys in 1914 but then in 1915 took command of the 82nd Infantry Brigade.

The Battle of Jutland took place in the North Sea off the coast of Denmark. Proving to be the biggest engagement at sea during the First World War, the battle brought together the world's two most powerful naval forces of the time: the British Grand High Fleet and the German High Seas Fleet. Britain had the larger fleet with 150 vessels to Germany's 99, but it was Britain that would suffer the heaviest casualties with 6,097 men killed to Germany's 2,551.

HMS *Indefatigable* was a larger version of the earlier *Invincible*-class battle-cruiser built in 1909 and launched on 28 October of that year. A telegram from the fleet to the Admiralty on 2 June 1916 told that at 3.50pm on 31 May 1916 the battle-cruiser fleet reported its engagement with the enemy. Ten minutes after the start of that engagement *Indefatigable* was reported to have sunk, having taken a hit from enemy fire by a shell exploding in its magazine (ammunition storage area).

## Missiles and Malaria

However, not all of those who did not survive the war died from wounds received in battle. It wasn't just the machine-gun fire, bayonets and shells the soldiers had to worry about. Disease was rife and could quickly spread to incapacitate many men. Dysentery, tuberculosis, typhoid, malaria, body lice and trench-foot to name but a few were the scourge of men in the trenches. For example, Private Charles Angell died on 27 March 1918 from tuberculosis in England and Ordinary Seaman William Barlow also died in the UK in February 1918 from meningitis.

Local man Dick Andrews serving abroad, seen here on his camel. (*Courtesy of Shropshire County Museum Service*)

Another local man, T.G. Hodnett, in Egypt. (*Courtesy of Shropshire County Museum Service*)

T.G. Hodnett on horseback. (*Courtesy of Shropshire County Museum Service*)

Not even Mayor Sheldon, who was mayor of Ludlow twice (1902–04 and 1917–21), was immune from the tragedy of war as his son Edward died on 24 February 1919. The family also ran the Horse and Jockey public house in Old Street. Edward was a sergeant in the Royal Garrison Artillery and died of tuberculosis. His grave is in St Leonard's Cemetery, Ludlow.

The men from Ludlow who fought ended up in many different battalions and regiments across all the theatres of war. From Arras to Loos, Passchendaele and Ypres, there was a Ludlow man fighting and, sadly, dying. By the end of 1914, 1,186,337 men had enlisted in Britain. Of these, there were around 89,000 British casualties.

**A Family Affair**
It was not uncommon for several members of the same family to be

fighting in the trenches or at sea at any one time. One such family was the Saunders. Alfred and Elizabeth Saunders of Rock Cottage Dairy, Lower Galdeford had four sons in the armed forces: Alfred, Geoffrey, George and Philip. They emigrated to Canada somewhere between 1909 and 1913.

Alfred enlisted on 8 November 1915 at Toronto Recruiting Depot into the 109th Regiment, 84th C.S. Battalion. He embarked on the *Empress of Britain* on 18 June 1916. The *Empress of Britain* was an armed merchant ship and was launched on 11 November 1905. She was commissioned by the navy in August 1915 for troop transport and returned to civilian duties in 1915 before being broken up in 1930.

Alfred Saunders. (*Courtesy of the Saunders family*)

On 30 June 1916 he was transferred to the 75th Infantry Battalion and trained at Bramshott Camp. From there he was sent on active service to Le Havre in August 1916. It is known that he caught a train to Steenvoorde, Belgium on 12 August 1916 where he was soon on a route march to the front: Poperinghe and then to the south section of the Ypres Salient on 13 August.

He was engaged in heavy fighting under the Messines Ridge and Hellfire Corner until 18 September 1916 when certain divisions were withdrawn to the Somme. Messines Ridge was a stronghold to the south-east of Ypres and had been a small German salient from early 1914. The preparations that Alfred and his comrades were making in 1916 were to pave the way for a successful battle and takeover here in 1917.

Hellfire Corner was once considered 'the most dangerous corner on Earth' as it intersected with the Menin Road, an important junction, and was under heavy surveillance by the German army who attacked anything that came along it.

Alfred then saw action at the Somme, Thiepval Ridge and Wood and was involved in the Battle of Ancre Heights in October 1916. In the Regina Trench attack where they saw a 50 per cent casualty rate the troops were forced to withdraw from the little ground they had gained; however, the trench was regained in November 1916. Later on there were no trenches left; the area was just a quagmire of mud and shell-holes.

On Christmas Eve 1916 Alfred moved with his division to the trenches under Vimy Ridge to hold the ground and prepare for the coming attack in April. Tunnels were dug deep into the chalk ground with frequent trench raids to the German trenches at night.

Although he had escaped relatively unscathed until then, his luck was about to run out in 1917 when they tried out some new gas called phosgene which the soldiers carried in 90lb tanks on their backs. Due to some of the nozzles being faulty and leaking gas, Alfred found himself in hospital seven times suffering from the effects of this gas.

Phosgene, a colourless gas with the smell of musty hay, was thought to have been first used by the Germans in December 1915. It was highly toxic and the effects could take two days or more to show. Immediate effects could be coughing with lung and eye irritation. Ultimately it often led to a build-up of fluid in the lungs and subsequent death. Up to 85 per cent of the 91,000 deaths in the war from gas were estimated to be from phosgene gas, although some gases were used in combination. Alfred died on 1 March 1917 following a gas attack and machine-gun fire on Vimy Ridge. He was among 600 men lost in that attack.

Although a great many men died during the Great War, it is important to remember that many also survived and returned home. The Charmers were a family who had members die and some who survived the war and they still have relatives living in Ludlow today.

James Charmer was born in Naghead Yard, Corve Street in 1891. He married Mary Thronton and had six children. When war broke out he enlisted in Hereford in the Royal Horse Artillery. His name is carved on the Ludford Memorial.

Another family member to enlist was Charles Charmer who was born in Ludlow in 1883 to his unmarried mother Elizabeth Charmer. By trade he was a baker at Price's in Ludlow and he later married Emily Reynalds. They had one son, Wallace. Charles served in the Pre-Army Service Corps and landed in France in July 1915. He survived the war to return home.

Charles Charmer. (*Courtesy of Margaret Edwards and Jean Parker*)

Geoffrey, George and Philip Saunders and brother-in-law William Miles. (*Courtesy of the Saunders family*)

James Charmer. (*Courtesy of Margaret Edwards and Jean Parker*)

William Henry Charmer Jnr was also born in Ludlow in 1899. He was the son of William and Alice Charmer, a private in the 1st Battalion, East Lancashire Regiment. Unfortunately he died aged just 17 on 7 April 1916 and his grave is in Doullens Communal Cemetery.

In this extract taken from a letter written to his mother, William appears to be revelling in his new-found role:

> I have landed safely. We travelled all night on Monday ... we got here at half past 11 on Tuesday. I have been inoculated ... we are billeted out and am having a jolly good time of it but I don't think you are. We have got our uniform. I look like Lord Roberts ... You have no need to trouble about me as you bet as I'll watch having any ale or being down in the dumps ... I have had no time to write before now but don't think about me because I am going alright.

William Charmer.
(*Courtesy of Margaret Edwards and Jean Parker*)

However, later on his brave resolve seemed to waver as homesickness appears to have crept in as shown by this subsequent letter: 'Did you get that last letter I sent, because it puts me crazy when I can't hear from you. Have you had a bilious turn or something ... I begin crying to myself when I don't hear from you.'

Charles Thomas Tipton, born in 1896 in Bromfield, Ludlow also has relatives in Ludlow today but was not one of the first to go to war, being in an exempted occupation at the time. However, eventually he was called up and had only been in France for ten days when he was discharged, possibly due to the effects of a gas attack. Charles was a gunner with the Royal Field Artillery, having enlisted on 31 January 1916 at the age of 19 years and 11 months, and was a farm labourer living at 21 Lower Haven Lane, Ludlow at the time.

Before the war started, he had married Alice and they had a son, Jim, who was sadly drowned in the local river, the Teme, aged 15. Like many men who came back from the war he never really talked about his experiences to his family but he did say that he remembered falling

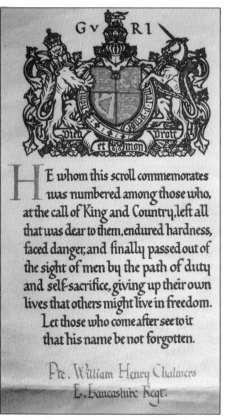

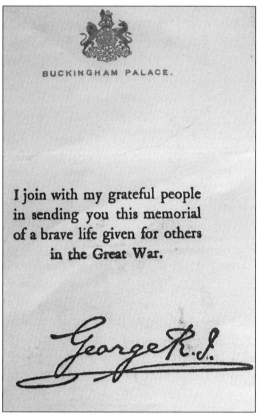

Scroll commemorating William's death. (*Courtesy of Margaret Edwards and Jean Parker*)

The king's memorial certificate sent to families whose loved ones had been killed. (*Courtesy of Margaret Edwards and Jean Parker*)

As above from Lord Kitchener. (*Courtesy of Margaret Edwards and Jean Parker*) down in the trenches into water during a gas attack. When he came round he was in a military hospital in Aldershot and couldn't remember anything about how he got from the trenches to Aldershot. He was no stranger to hospitals, having also been admitted to a Red Cross hospital in Canada, and was discharged in 1918.

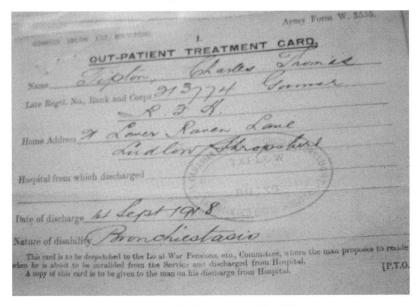

Charles Tipton's outpatients card. (*Courtesy of Fred Tipton*)

Life when he returned home was not easy, for the gas had left his lungs badly damaged. He would rise in the morning, go down to the garden gate and cough for ten minutes or more. He had contracted bronchiectasis, a lung disease. Prior to the war he had worked on Clive of India's local estate at Bromfield but he didn't want to return there after coming home. He then joined the railway and was the fireman on the steam trains travelling between Crewe and Cardiff but was dismissed from this job due to a minor train crash caused by him. He then went back to work for Clive of India in the saw mill where he worked until he died at the age of 52 in Ludlow Cottage Hospital of heart failure and bronchiectasis.

Life was similarly difficult for many ex-servicemen returning home. Despite reassurances and promises from the government and employers, many men returned to find their old jobs gone and those

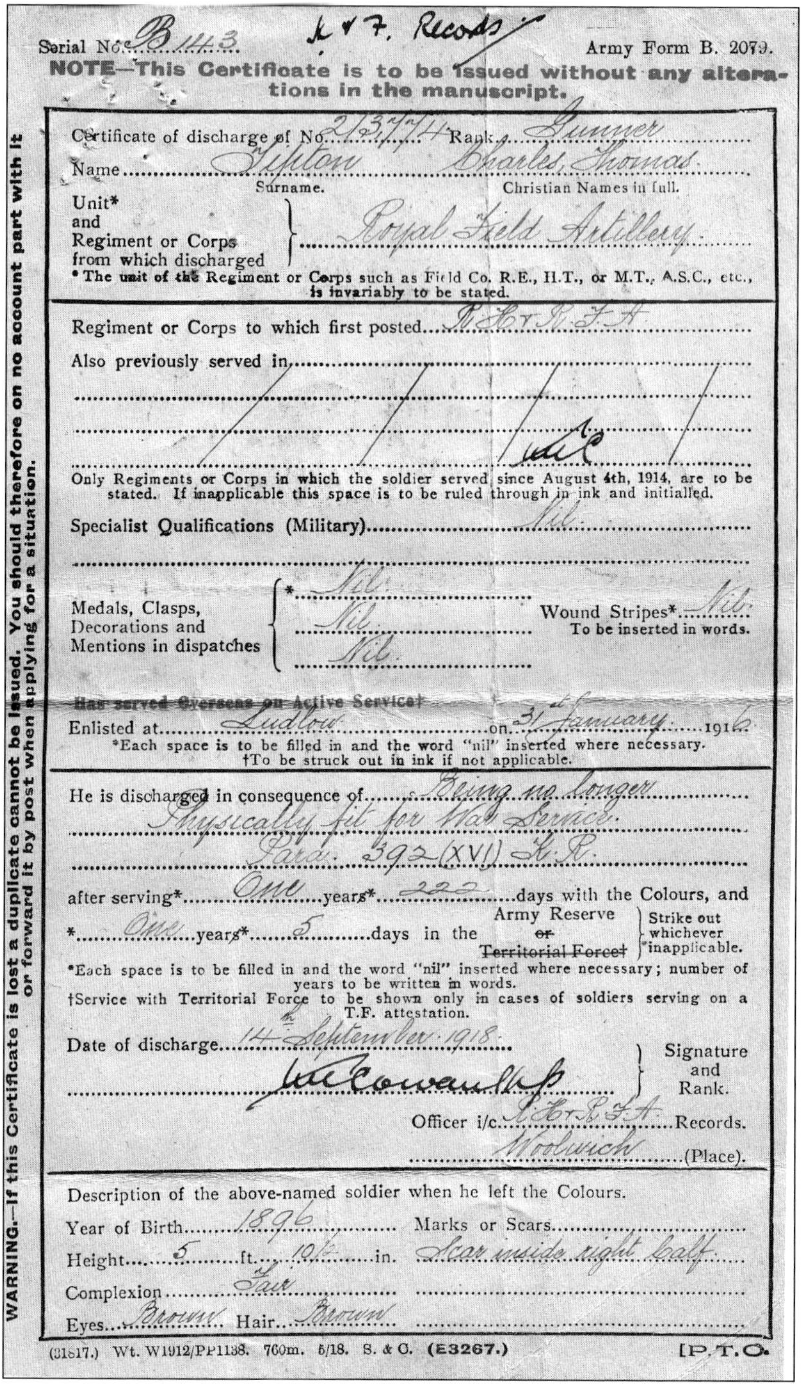

Serial No. B 1143. R & 7. Records Army Form B. 2079.

**NOTE—This Certificate is to be issued without any alterations in the manuscript.**

Certificate of discharge of No. 213774 Rank Gunner

Name Tipton Charles Thomas
Surname. Christian Names in full.

Unit* and Regiment or Corps from which discharged } Royal Field Artillery

* The unit of the Regiment or Corps such as Field Co. R.E., H.T., or M.T., A.S.C., etc., is invariably to be stated.

Regiment or Corps to which first posted R.H. & R.F.A.

Also previously served in ........ / / / / Nil

Only Regiments or Corps in which the soldier served since August 4th, 1914, are to be stated. If inapplicable this space is to be ruled through in ink and initialled.

Specialist Qualifications (Military) Nil

Medals, Clasps, Decorations and Mentions in dispatches { * Nil / Nil / Nil

Wound Stripes* Nil. To be inserted in words.

~~Has served Overseas on Active Service†~~

Enlisted at Ludlow on 31st January 1916

*Each space is to be filled in and the word "nil" inserted where necessary.
†To be struck out in ink if not applicable.

He is discharged in consequence of Being no longer Physically fit for War Service. Para. 392 (XVI) K.R.

after serving* One years* 222 days with the Colours, and

* One years* 5 days in the Army Reserve ~~or Territorial Force†~~ } Strike out whichever inapplicable.

*Each space is to be filled in and the word "nil" inserted where necessary; number of years to be written in words.
†Service with Territorial Force to be shown only in cases of soldiers serving on a T.F. attestation.

Date of discharge 14th September 1918.

[signature] } Signature and Rank.

Officer i/c R.H. & R.F.A. Records.

Woolwich (Place).

Description of the above-named soldier when he left the Colours.

Year of Birth 1896 Marks or Scars Scar inside right calf

Height 5 ft. 10½ in.

Complexion Fair

Eyes Brown Hair Brown

(31817.) Wt. W1912/PP1138. 760m. 5/18. S. & C. (E3267.) [P.T.O.

WARNING.—If this Certificate is lost a duplicate cannot be issued. You should therefore on no account part with it or forward it by post when applying for a situation.

Charles Tipton's discharge papers. (*Courtesy of Fred Tipton*)

Reference No. 9/MT 3086

MINISTRY OF PENSIONS,

MINISTRY OF PENSIONS,
WEST MIDLANDS REGION.
AWARDS SECTION,
LIONEL STREET,
1 6 MAR 1923    BIRMINGHAM
......................192....

SIR,

I am directed by the Minister of Pensions to inform you that he has reviewed your case, and has issued instructions to the Pension Issue Office for payment of the following amended award. The amount awarded is in accordance with the assessment of your condition at your last Board.

| Weekly Rate. | | From | To | Remarks |
|---|---|---|---|---|
| MAN. | Allowance for wife and/or children. | | | |
| s. d. | s. d. | | | |
| 9 . 6 | included | 21. 2. 23 | for 10 weeks | Final Weekly alle |
| Plus £20.0.0 (twenty pounds) | | terminal | gratuity | |
| | | payable only at end of period | | |
| Subject to deduction | of award notified 9.2.23 | | | |

Under the provisions of the Royal Warrant of 1919 this award is liable to readjustment in and after the year 1923 according to the increase or decrease in the cost of living.

Any further correspondence regarding the amount or duration of this award should be directed to the address given above and should quote the reference number stated in the left hand top corner of this communication. Any complaints regarding stoppage of payment of pension due to non-receipt of Ring Paper or non-arrival of Book of Drafts at the Post Office should be addressed to :—

The Ministry of Pensions,
Pension Issue Office,
Bromyard Avenue,
Acton, London, W.3.,

stating your full name, address, regimental particulars, and the reference number on your latest Ring Paper.

I am, Sir,

Your obedient Servant,

Mr. Chas. Thos. Tipton
Mill House Bromfield
Ludlow. Salop.

M.P.A. 5/3

B. V. SYDENHAM

REGIONAL DIRECTOR

Charles Tipton's pension letter. (*Courtesy of Fred Tipton*)

Charles Tipton's war medals: (left) campaign medal known as 'Pip'; (centre) British War Medal known as 'Squeak'; and (right) Allied Victory Medal known as 'Wilfred' (around 5.7 million of this medal were issued). The Pip, Squeak and Wilfred were named after characters in a *Daily Mail* cartoon from 1920. Pip was a dog, Squeak was a penguin and Wilfred was a rabbit. (*Courtesy of Fred Tipton*)

who had been discharged from the army had to rely on pensions as shown by this letter dated 23 March 1923 regarding Charles Tipton's pension.

Another soldier, Gilbert Williams, served in the KSLI and also has relatives in Ludlow today. He was shot in the stomach and his son recollected the first time he saw the wound and asked his father about it. The latter rarely talked about his experiences but one of them was outlined in a letter he received in the 1960s from a fellow soldier on the 'never to be forgotten anniversary':

Gilbert Williams. (*Courtesy of Stanley Williams*)

I often think of the working parties we went on, heavily loaded with boxes of rations of the old soldiers who left us to carry them three parts of the way and appeared to give us our rifles. Of the night of 13th July when we were spread out in No Man's Land, waiting for the attack to commence, how a mouse was so terrified at the noise of the bombardment that it ran up my sleeve. I'm sure I was as frightened as the mouse. We were only lads of 19 then, Gilbert. I am sure it is only providence that saved us from death. Now after 48 years it comes back in our memory and we live it all over again.

Gilbert reminisced to his son about a night when his battalion was in no man's land, trying out a new tactic. On their way to the enemy trenches they were confronted by a thicket of grass and thistles which afforded them some cover. Even though it was night and they had this cover, Gilbert thought the Germans could sense that they were hiding there. Prior to this there had been a terrific bombardment – the one described in the letter – which was intended to flatten the barbed-wire fencing so they could get through. They were waiting for dawn to complete the raid and when the whistles were blown signalling the start of the raid, they charged.

He said that when he got up to run he could feel the next man close to him but as they reached the wire they found it still standing. A dum-dum bullet ripped through his abdomen. His son Stanley remembered when his dad was getting dressed he could see a thumbnail-sized hole in his abdomen that grew to an exit wound on his back that you could put your fist into.

Army Form B. 2079.

**WARNING.**—*If you lose this Certificate a duplicate cannot be issued.*

Certificate of discharge of No. *1961* (Rank) *Private*

(Name) *Gilbert Williams*

(Regiment) **KING'S SHROPSHIRE L. I.**

who was enlisted at *Ludlow*

on the *22nd Nov.* 19*15*.

Section of Gilbert Williams' discharge papers. (*Courtesy of Stanley Williams*)

Even though men such as Gilbert and Charles survived, they were often left with devastating injuries and scars, both mental and physical. Such men were often subject to jibes and harassment from people in the street when they were discharged, being mistaken for shirkers or those who had failed to enlist. The government eventually issued war badges to be worn by ex-servicemen who had been discharged to show that they had already done their duty for king and country.

Gilbert Williams' war badge. (*Courtesy of Stanley Williams*)

Charles Tipton's war badge certificate. (*Courtesy of Fred Tipton*)

Another local man joined the navy. His name was William John Mantle. Born in October 1896 in Bitterley, near Ludlow, he lived at Titterstone Cottages and was a quarryman. He volunteered on 12 August 1916 and served aboard the *Arlanza*.

The *Arlanza*. (*Courtesy of Margory Sheldon*)

The *Arlanza* was an armed merchant cruiser built in 1912 but not taken into naval service until 1915 and could hold up to 1,390 passengers. When commissioned by the navy, she was converted and had six 6-inch guns. The ship had an unfortunate encounter with a German ship in August 1914 when she was ordered to stop. When it was ascertained that the ship had women and children on board they were allowed to carry on about their business. However, the ship later suffered damage to her hull from a mine.

William was just 17 when war broke out and he enlisted in the navy. He won £9 for his part in preventing an armament of explosives being smuggled underneath a cargo of onions during the war.

Wartime wasn't all mine-dodging and high alert. In 1918, William took part in a 'dunking' ceremony as he crossed the equator.

Even though there was some fun to be had, he also witnessed the tragedy that resulted from a collision between two ammunition ships at Halifax, Nova Scotia. This incident saw 1,900 fatalities with a further 9,000 people injured.

After the war both William Mantle and Gilbert Williams attended the 1919 Peace Day celebrations in Ludlow as shown in the photograph on page 54.

William Mantle survived the war and returned to Ludlow where he first worked at a quarry and then for the railway. Despite the mines, the hardship of serving in the navy and the horrors he had witnessed, William lived to the grand old age of 95.

William Mantle's Certificate of Service. (*Courtesy of Margory Sheldon*)

William Mantle in uniform. (*Courtesy of Margory Sheldon*)

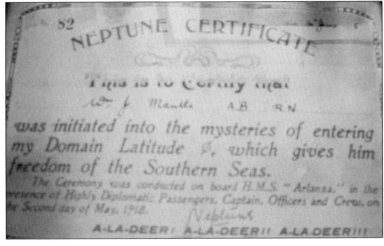

William Mantle's Neptune Certificate. (*Courtesy of Margory Sheldon*)

Both Gilbert Williams (second row, fifth from right) and William Mantle (third row, fourth from left) can be seen in this photo. (*Courtesy of Margory Sheldon*)

From the small parish of Stanton Lacy, 4 miles from Ludlow, 123 men went to war with 101 of them returning. The Lewis family of four brothers was one such family. Richard Lewis joined the KSLI on 9 August 1915. He became a sergeant but did not survive the war and his memorial is at the Menin Gate. His brother Thomas also joined the KSLI in 1918 and also did not survive; his memorial is at Arras. Walter was the next brother to enlist and he became a corporal, receiving the DCM (Distinguished Conduct Medal) for taking charge of his platoon when his commander was injured, making the journey to establish a post under intense shell and machine-gun fire. It is clear that it was a rare Ludlow family that was untouched by the devastation of war.

# CHAPTER 5

# Agriculture

*'But who will find them food to eat?'*

Ludlow is surrounded by some of the most beautiful and fertile agricultural land in Great Britain, so it is little wonder that during the war the land and those who worked it would play a big part in the war effort.

In fact, one of the local papers of the time, the *WJ*, in its 8 August issue told of the 'great excitement' contained within the Ludlow Company of the Territorials and C Squadron of the Shropshire Yeomanry headquarters in Ludlow as the smartly-dressed farmers' sons paraded into town along with their horses. It must have been a wondrous sight for the townspeople to see so many of their brave, local lads from the farming community coming to volunteer to fight for their king and country. The newspaper stated it was 'such a sight as had never been witnessed' in the town before.

The local community was not backward in coming forward to offer up accommodation for their billeting either, with several of the local inns and hotels being made available for that purpose before the men were given their orders to go on to Barry Docks in Wales and marched through the town to the railway station.

Before they left, the Mayor of Ludlow, Councillor S.H. Valentine, gave an address in which he said that 'he knew that if they should unfortunately, in one sense, meet the enemy, they would do their duty and do great honour to themselves and Ludlow.'

As the war progressed and more and more farmers' sons and workers were compelled to enlist, this left the nation's farmers with a problem. With fewer men to tend to the livestock, harvest time approaching and with many of their horses and vehicles having been requisitioned by the military, it became apparent that they would struggle to bring in the harvest.

Farmers were beginning to seriously feel the effects of war. While on the one hand they were expected to carry on producing food for the country – the need for which, in a few years' time due to blockades by German U-boats, would increase exponentially – they no longer had the manpower to do so. Another issue affecting manpower was the Irish workers who were returning home and enlisting in their home regiments.

This little rhyme of the period demonstrates the concerns about the farmers' plight and where food supplies were going to come from:

> There's a crowd of little children
> That march along and shout,
> For it's fine to play at soldiers
> Now their fathers are called out;
> So it's beat, drums, beat;
> But who will find them food to eat?

However, lack of manpower wasn't the only thing giving farmers sleepless nights. One of the main things to affect agriculture was the weather, as had been the case since farmers first took to the land. It had always been one of the main topics of conversation and national interest and wartime was no exception. In fact, the weather became a lot more than a topic of local gossip. Now, more than ever before, it became a 'save or starve' situation.

Reports were that the weather of August, September and October 1914 had been more than favourable to the farmer and his crops. In fact, one report even went so far as to point out that the war, from an agricultural point of view, couldn't have come at a more opportune moment.

Other reports causing concern to farmers at the time were those of rising wheat prices and how long the numbers of crops that farmers were presently able to produce would last if the war was to continue for any substantial length of time. If prices continued to rise, how long would their customers be able to afford to eat?

The scale of this conflict at a time when Britain was so dependent on imports had never been seen before, so agriculturists were unsure how long the supplies of home-produced food would last. The harvest would have to be good; all signs indicated that it would be, but the harvests of the allies from whom Great Britain could still obtain imports might be less so.

### Feeding the Nation

Agriculture was one of the major industries and employers in the town. With the vast acreage of arable land in the area, it was both a profitable but also a back-breaking concern. The land was laid open to cereal crops such as corn and wheat and the farming of livestock, particularly cattle. There was also a thriving market catering for the local community.

The rural idyll that many seek today bears little resemblance to the hardships borne by farmers, tenants and farm labourers during wartime. Farming was hard work and they were at the mercy of the elements. A wet, cold summer was bad news for the farmer because it affected the quality and quantity of the crops, leading to shortages and price increases for the consumer. The dependency of the farmer on the land and the weather would be all the more crucial in the years to come. The state of the harvest was critical in wartime, especially for an island nation such as Britain.

Just before the war, the Boards of Agriculture and Education produced a white paper which was the report of the Rural Education Conference, detailing their recommendations for developing the skills of those employed in agriculture. Older boys and girls attending rural elementary schools were to be instructed in manual agricultural labour. The school holidays were structured so as to allow the boys to work the land and help get the harvest in. There was agreement that this manual instruction would be provided by the local education authorities. However, in the years to come, the problem would be that many of the local lads working the farms would go off to fight, leaving a deficiency of skilled labour.

**The Plight of the Farmer**
However, all was not well at the time. This letter printed in the *WJ* of 11 July 1914 gives some idea of the plight of the farm labourer at the time:

> Although £1 a week cannot be called good wages ... every able-bodied farm labourer ought to get £1 a week and his cottage and garden free and may I add that it might be quite possible to arrange for each man to stop work at one o'clock once a fortnight, but how can this be done as long as under our present system our farmers are unfairly treated by the importation of duty-free agricultural produce from all over the world, whilst our own products are so heavily taxed?

Contrary to government reassurances about sufficient food being available, the general public was not so sure. In fact, in the week of 22 August the Higher Education Committee discussed the possible shortage of food for that winter and advised that it would be 'desirable' to encourage cottages and other homes to produce what they could. In order to make sure the quality of food was good, plans were laid for 'practical cookery instruction' in every parish and hamlet across the country.

The Lord Lieutenant of Shropshire (the Earl of Powis) also tried to reassure the people of Shropshire regarding a potential food crisis caused by the war. A committee was appointed to oversee food production and was further divided into smaller local committees for the day-to-day business; these would comprise three or four 'prominent' ladies, one of whom should be a 'lady of influence and position'.

The Board of Agriculture and Fisheries also appointed an Agricultural Executive Committee of Food Supplies to look at the status of food supplies across the country. Although they fully understood that farmers were at a disadvantage due to their skilled workers going off to fight, something had to be done to increase food production. They had plans to help alleviate the deficit by trying to obtain suitably skilled workers via the Labour Exchange.

In the first few months of the war harvest time was fast approaching and if the country wanted to avert a potential disaster in terms of food supplies they were going to have to address the lack of skilled workers in the fields. Because of the difficulty in finding the right skilled labour, local landowners were asked to second some of their workers to help the farmers bring in the harvest. Always ready and eager to help, once again the scouts took up the call to assist; they were asked to carry messages between farmers and landowners and could also provide a potential source of labour.

## The Backbone of Britain

Even Lord Kitchener recognized the value and importance of rural districts such as Ludlow and was eager to engage their support: 'I rely confidently on the rural population of all grades, to perform its share of the national duty at this crisis in our history.'

The government recognized that farmers and landowners were the 'backbone of Britain' and the Empire and that they were being relied upon in their nation's hour of need. How the crops grew now and throughout the war would be key to ensuring food supplies. After all, food was just as important to the war effort as munitions. There would be little by way of supplies from abroad to help if the harvest failed. With the ongoing conflict in France, Belgium and other areas and those countries' own farm workers engaged in the fighting, their own harvests would be affected. To make matters worse, once the Germans laid their mines and engaged their U-boats, cargos of imports were liable to loss at sea.

## Grow Your Own

Of significance to farmers early on in the war was the notice that the military authorities would be looking out for large amounts of market garden and farm produce for use by the troops. Farmers were once more called upon to help the government and the war effort by declaring how much they could offer and sell at a fair price.

As the war progressed, farmers would play a part in food production on a much larger scale than ever before. Early on in the conflict, there was much talk about the utilization of allotments to help prevent shortages. The Board of Agriculture and Fisheries planned to encourage more allotment cultivation to help provide additional foodstuffs. There would be technical advisors from agricultural colleges to give instruction about how to get the best yield from

Harper Adams Agricultural College. (*Courtesy of Harper Adams Agricultural University*)

Tractor training for women at Harper Adams Agricultural College. (*Courtesy of Harper Adams Agricultural University*)

allotments and what to plant, etc. With Harper Adams Agricultural College about 40 miles up the road, it was inevitable that they would play a big part in this initiative, including training the first Land Girls.

Apart from working hard to increase food production, farmers were also engaged in charity work, raising money via jumble sales. By April 1916 they had raised £65,000 for Allied Farmers. In Ludlow in 1915 the South Shropshire Farmers' Union held an auction of agricultural equipment and animals that had been donated; the auction raised £147.

Landowners were also asked to donate land for allotments, free of taxes and rent for a year. The local committees would provide seedlings and see to it that any person with free time would assist in the maintenance and running of the allotments. It wasn't long before they considered ploughing up the racecourse – now a racecourse and golf course – for growing vegetables, and German PoWs who were accommodated on the site would be helping to plough up Ludford Park for the same purpose.

Ludlow racecourse and golf course today. (*Author's own*)

As above. (*Author's own*)

The Food Hoarding Order also came into force in April 1915. It wasn't long before one local establishment – Castle Lodge in The Square, Ludlow – was ordered to pay £24 in fines and costs and saw half their sugar and tea supplies taken away. They had 129lb 8oz of sugar! Food and the fair distribution of it were high on the agenda.

At one point in April 1915 the future of the Ludlow Agricultural Show was in doubt as it was discussed whether it should be stopped in light of the war. However, the organizers were concerned that if the show did not go ahead they would lose subscriptions. The chairman at the time thought it would be a 'great mistake' not to hold it: 'Nothing did more good to a farming district than an agricultural exhibition.' However, not everyone on the committee shared his views and the show would be temporarily abandoned later on in the war years. Another member was adamant that it shouldn't be held at a time when Ludlow was grieving for its lost men and that it was wrong to host or attend any kind of entertainment.

Generally the feeling was one of 'business as usual'. In a farming community that had already lost many men and horses to the war and with the prospect of losing many more, the show would be a boost to morale and show people that although there was a war in progress, Ludlow was still capable of staying afloat and wouldn't be beaten by the conflict.

**Save or Starve**
By late November 1916, one of the first new food regulations came into force in Ludlow by way of an order fixing the price of milk and flour. The milling order stipulated the percentage of flour that should be extracted from wheat. The hoarding of white flour became illegal in January 1916.

In December 1916 the Board of Trade made an order to regulate meals in restaurants and hotels and any other public place where people might eat. Courses were limited to three between 6pm and 9.30pm but two courses at all other times. There was also talk of there being meatless days after Christmas on one day per week. Although this would be difficult to monitor and enforce, the authorities made it known that it would be people's patriotic duty to comply. Further food regulations came into force later that month with the introduction of the so-called 'war loaf'. Such loaves were of smaller size than usual, contained less flour and potatoes were sometimes used as an ingredient to make up for the flour reduction. Although some were concerned about the quality of the bread, when it actually went into production there were no complaints at the time.

Concerns about food production and reducing waste were gathering pace and included a discussion by Ludlow Town Council about whether the local byelaws regarding keeping pigs could be relaxed to allow more members of the local community to keep their own pigs. They also suggested that pigs should be fed scraps to save food wastage and that previously uncultivated land and gardens could be used for food production. The council would provide seeds, etc. for this purpose.

As part of this initiative, the Ludlow Guild of Toymakers was closed from Saturday, 24 March 1917 for six weeks so that they could cultivate their gardens for food production. Readers of the *LA* were eagerly coming forward with their tips on how to reduce food wastage too. One reader suggested boiling potatoes in their skins and re-using tea and coffee grounds.

Alderman Sheldon said of food production in the town that 'It would be a disgrace to the town and to that council if the gardens were left uncultivated at a time when food was so much needed for the nation.' To that end a committee was formed to help coordinate the food production efforts of the town.

By March 1917 there was a shortfall of the potato crop and many people in Ludlow had to do without their roast potatoes with Sunday lunch. There were reports of potato-sellers profiteering in the town by trying to charge more than the regulated price and that the police had become involved.

One local farmer who was fined for charging over the agreed fixed price was Charles Bobb from Orleton Common. He claimed not to have realized that such an order was in force and that he couldn't afford to sell them at such a low price. He was given short shrift and told he could be fined £100 under DORA regulations, but he got away with a £15 fine including costs.

Even the mayor was at it! Mr Valentine had a grocer's shop in town and it was alleged that he had sold 2lb of potatoes at 2d per lb to two customers. He admitted that he'd done it and was fined 15s in each case. However, with the speed of change and new regulations popping up left, right and centre, people could possibly be excused for pleading confusion and ignorance.

British Summer Time, also known as Daylight Saving, was introduced in 1917 in an attempt to save fuel and money. Britain was going all out to find ways of conserving, restricting and eking out her resources; our performance in the war and the country's very survival depended on it.

One reader of the *LA* made the suggestion that the River Teme that flowed through the town could be used to power increased food production as it flowed through 'one of the largest agricultural and fruit growing districts in England'. The thinking was that the power of the mills and weirs could be used to grind the corn.

As concerns grew about the lack of food, a voluntary rationing scheme was introduced in March 1917. The idea was for cheaper foodstuffs such as bread and potatoes to be saved for the poor and that general food consumption should be reduced. The War Savings committees were to mount a national campaign as requested by the Ministry of Food.

Shropshire had its own War Agricultural Committee whose job it was to organize the changes required of agriculture in the county. In November 1917 they made it known that they could loan horses to farmers for use by their ploughmen. This, although seemingly a small gesture, could mean the difference between a good and a bad harvest and was therefore deemed essential to the war effort.

In order to create space to increase food production, in May 1917 another 100,000 acres of pasture land in Shropshire would need to be ploughed. Some 175 tons of seed potatoes had already been distributed and fifteen tractors were working across the county, including one driven by Maud Jones of Whitley Farm, near Newport.

The Food Controller stated in April 1917 that 'Every crumb should be saved, and the person who eats a slice of bread more than he needs, the servant who throws away a crust, the housewife who fails to exercise the most careful supervision over the rationing of her household is helping the enemy.'

By December 1917 'Save or Starve' had become Great Britain's motto, with a whole week devoted to encouraging people to make further sacrifices to reduce food consumption.

In January 1918 the Food Control Joint Advisory Committee met

Maud Jones driving one of the first tractors in Shropshire. (*Courtesy of Brian Watson Jones*)

to look at the price of butter, milk and bread and how these would be distributed. It was decided that butter would be fixed at 2s 6d per lb. To save flour, potatoes would be used in the bread-making process and the committee had bought 4 tons. Those producing and selling milk were finding times hard but the committee decided to keep to the going rate of 5½d per quart delivered. Bread was to be sold by weight.

The Shropshire War Agricultural Executive Committee was also coming down hard in January 1918. It threatened that those who had already been given notice to plough and cultivate their land but did not commence before the following week would incur enforcement proceedings. This would not be an easy task with the cold, snowy weather.

By January 1918, it wasn't just potatoes that were scarce: one pub had to close its doors over a weekend because it ran out of beer. Applications forms were sent out to people in the borough of Ludlow and Craven Arms in March 1918 so they could apply for food rationing cards. What had been voluntary was now being enforced. Meat rationing coupons and ration cards for butter, margarine and tea were sent out to householders.

Long queues were to be seen as locals headed to the food control offices in Church Street, Ludlow on Monday and Tuesday in early April 1918 as people made applications for sugar to use in jam-making. In the same month the butchers ran out of meat and were closed on the Monday. Because they were also closed as normal for the next two days [reason unknown and unexplained in local newspaper source], the people of Ludlow had to wait till the Thursday before they could use their meat coupons.

When one considers the meagre rations on which the troops existed, the least those at home could do was tighten their belts and ensure there was enough food to go round. It was noted that women would be the focal point for ensuring the success of the scheme and women's societies would be giving out advice on rationing and frugality. The rich were the target this time; it was felt that until they had made some sacrifices it would be unfair to ask the poor, who already lived a hand-to-mouth existence, to make reductions. Those who took part in the scheme were given cards to display in their windows which read: 'In honour bound we adopt the national scale of voluntary rations.' The Food Controller, ever keen to encourage people to reduce wastage, said: 'If every person will eat another pound of bread less per week, we can laugh at the submarines.'

It wasn't long before communal or community kitchens were set up in the town. There was one at 2 Old Street that opened on Tuesdays and Wednesdays to prepare meals for the local schoolchildren. Tickets were sold at 2d each and seventy tickets were taken in one week. It was made clear that this wasn't a soup kitchen or a charity: it was merely to help avoid waste and to reduce the consumption of bread, as well as ensuring that the local children would have a decent meal for at least two days a week.

A month later, by February 1918, they were serving over 100 meals a week with some people having to be turned away. It was hoped to increase their capacity as soon as possible and by the end of February 1918 they were serving 150 meals a week.

A public meeting in the Town Hall about food production and the economy campaign was scheduled for mid-February 1918; there were to be speakers from the National League of Safety and Rowland Hunt MP would participate.

There was also a special exhibition held in the Town Hall in June

Old Street, where the war kitchen was based, 2015. (*Author's own*)

1918. The theme of this exhibition was food production and saving food. There were cookery displays, demonstrations on food-bottling, drying and preserving, among other tips. There was no excuse for the people of Ludlow not to do their utmost to reduce waste and eat frugally.

When changes were made to the exemption rules regarding military service, as they were several times during the war, those involved in agriculture demanded that their workforce should be excluded due to the severe shortage of skilled men able to work the farms. It was understood that this work would mean sacrifice but that was deemed necessary and nothing compared to what the soldiers were experiencing abroad.

Thoughts were also turning to what would happen in agriculture when the war was over. It was suggested that increased food production should continue as a matter of national security. There would be a minimum wage set for farm labourers, wheat would have a fixed minimum price, imported food would carry a tariff, farms could be taken over by the government if they were deemed to be poorly managed and the shortage of farm workers' cottages would be remedied. Poor farming was viewed as being a hazard to the country.

September 1918 saw the introduction of new ration books and the locals had until 21 September to apply for them at 9 Church Street. Fuel was also running out and tips on saving fuel were issued by the Coal Controller. These included making the grate area of open fires smaller and repairing bricks in the flues of ranges. Coal dust could also be reused if it was dampened and formed into blocks, and the burning of vegetable and garden waste that couldn't be used to feed pigs was advised as well. Businesses in Ludlow closed earlier to help conserve coal. They closed at 6pm on Mondays, Tuesdays, Wednesdays and Fridays but could open until 8pm on Saturdays.

During the war years Ludlow was keen on its demonstrations and exhibitions. In September 1918 the Higher Education Department organized a war exhibition with dairy, poultry and garden products at the Town Hall. There were also to be demonstrations in the afternoon.

Despite rationing and food shortages, Ludlow still managed to send food parcels to PoWs interned abroad, and the sailors aboard HMS *Dragon*, HMS *Blonde* and HMS *Imperious*, among other ships, received fruit sent from Ludlow and were mighty glad to have it. There were also articles in the local paper about how to save food and these were well received. Even after the war had ended, rationing would continue for several years as the world of agriculture struggled to recover.

# CHAPTER 6

# Women's Work is Never Done

*'She bears up as best she can, patiently and without complaint.'*

The Great War was both a blessing and a curse for women. Many of them had jobs in service or families to care for, but the war suddenly saw them being thrown into the spotlight; this would change how they were viewed by society and their role within it. Many of their menfolk had gone away to war and they had no idea when they might see them again. News from the battlefields was scant at the best of times, open to rumour and confusion, and many women felt the pressure of the risk of losing their only income and, potentially, their homes. Who would take care of their interests with the main breadwinner gone?

However, this put women in a difficult position. They were expected to encourage their men to enlist and, judging from several letters in the local newspapers, they did this with aplomb, often attempting to shame those men still at home into enlisting. This was considered their patriotic duty, and their biggest movement – the Suffrage Movement – came under fire and was expected to stop its quest for the vote and equal rights at the outbreak of war.

**The Suffrage Movement**
In early July 1914 the Women's Suffrage Movement organized a

pilgrimage from 'the four corners of England' to a meeting in London. There were reports of huge crowds assembling, 'working towards the vote by all legal means available to them.' Although none of the four routes passed by Ludlow, those suffragettes from the town and across Shropshire who were able would have gone to show their support as the pilgrims marched down Watling Street in Wolverhampton.

An open-air meeting was held in Shropshire in August 1914 at which Mrs Harley of Condover and Miss Knight, the organizer of the West Midlands Federation, gave an address on the subject of women's suffrage. The meeting was well supported but the suffragettes, particularly as this country entered into war, were not admired by everyone as shown by the following letter in the local press:

> May I express my regret that so many women of my old country in the form of militant suffragettes should in their demand for the vote behave in such a deplorable way… It seems to me that if these English women desire to help to make laws they would be more successful if they were more law abiding.

Hopefully, by the end of the war, women had more than regained the letter-writer's respect by their patriotic and charitable conduct during the conflict.

Immediately after Mr Asquith had announced that Great Britain was at war with Germany, the Suffrage Movement wasted no time in its call to arms. A meeting was called in Wellington 'to make arrangements for organising help for those who will suffer from the effects of the war.'

The Great War was, in many ways, the catalyst that sparked a change in opinions and attitudes across many sectors of British life, including the way women were perceived in the workforce and home and other social changes. A poster in the local paper highlighted that a woman's work was never done. It ends with a poignant line describing the woman's lot during the First World War: 'She bears up as best she can, patiently and without complaint'; a precursor to the patriotic and 'can-do' attitude of women on the home front during the war. The local newspaper also spelled out the role and expectations of women as war broke out: 'Not only have they seen their sons, sweethearts and brothers don the khaki and vanish into the fighting ranks without murmuring, or more than tears shed in secret perhaps; but they have inspired their men-folk to do their duty.'

In August 1914 Mrs Henry Fawcett made a 'stirring' appeal to the National Union of Women and the suffrage societies to join together in order for them to better organize the aid the country would need if it was to get through the war. The suggestion that they should lay down their arms and activities of working towards their own goals of greater women's rights and the vote and instead concentrate on the plight of the country and alleviating the distress that the war would cause was met with open arms.

Within a week the women had made their 'prompt' response to Mrs Fawcett with over 1,000 applications for work registered. Many of those who applied, however, were professional and seeking paid employment; this was not within the remit of Mrs Fawcett's wishes as she was seeking volunteers. Those women who did want paid work were referred to the Labour Exchanges instead.

**Do Your Duty**
The women of Britain were now expected to put down their 'Votes for Women' banners and engage in the war, but the question was how? Some of the suggested activities suitable for women included helping on farms with the harvest, field work, boarding out young children, distributing government stores and money to reservists' families, Red Cross work, medical work and clerical work in offices set up for the emergency services. With Ludlow sitting in a prime agricultural area, it was inevitable that their attentions would soon be turned to working the land as we shall see in another chapter.

With the numbers of men signing up – and most of them being the sole breadwinner of the family – it would be natural for the women left behind to have to find work to keep their families going. Assurances from the government and some of the local landowners and employers that they would keep the soldiers' and sailors' jobs open until their return and help ease the financial burden of their families were treated with suspicion. Most people's minds were on the potential threat of the workhouse if they failed to keep their heads above water financially.

However, the war was something of a double-edged sword for women. Not only did it offer them opportunities in the workplace not normally available to them, it also caused problems with more traditional types of employment. Domestic service was one of the occupations to suffer as the war began to bite and the gentry were forced to let some of their staff go. None the less, there was a possible remedy for this problem and it came from the government of New South Wales offering work for British domestic servants who were well regarded over there. They were offered paid passage overseas and good wages; the more experienced workers would earn 12/6 to £1 a week. They used the premise that Australia was part of the Empire and was a healthy and 'attractive' place to live. There were also adverts aiming to entice British farmers to work on farms in Canada with the prospect of eventually owning their own place and settling there.

Yet was the offer as good as it appeared? It might seem appealing but would take women away from where they would soon be required in unprecedented numbers to work the land and take over other traditionally male-orientated occupations such as driving buses, working as office clerks and so on.

The efforts of women across the country, particularly in agriculture, caught the eye of the Earl of Selbourne, who was so impressed that he thought a Women's Roll of Honour should be set up to acknowledge their achievements. The idea of giving them a badge was considered. He was keen for women to be acknowledged for their part in the war effort, just as their menfolk were honoured for military service.

However, there was another issue more important to women and that was being given the vote, so long denied them. This point was highlighted in the local newspapers with a letter from the Suffragette Movement. They pointed out that both men and women had been working hard throughout the war and 'if service in His Majesty's forces during the present war is to be regarded as a voter's qualification it is quite impossible to leave them [women] out.'

This could have been seen as an attempt to use the war as leverage to obtain the vote for women, but the letter-writer was keen to point out that they did not see voting rights for women as a 'prize' for their war service. Women would eventually get their wish to vote, albeit with restrictions when it was first granted. However, it cannot be denied that the effort played by women in keeping the home fires burning for the duration of the war played no small part in winning them the vote.

Women's work during the war years was unprecedented in its nature and the women of Ludlow certainly had their mettle tested in many ways. Unfortunately for them and their counterparts all over the UK, many of their roles reverted back to those of the pre-war days as soon as the conflict ended and the men who had survived came back; however, their lives and standing in society would never be the same again.

**Sewing for Soldiers and Sailors**
Lord Kitchener might have been building his New Army of men to fight in the trenches but the Prince of Wales wanted his own army of women to head the fight against poverty on the home front, to make lives a little easier for those who would suffer great distress due to their menfolk going into military service. They soon got to work, as by the week of 15 August 1914 the National Relief Fund had already raised its first £million.

The local branch of the Queen Mary's Needlework Guild, a national initiative set up and endorsed by Queen Mary in 1914, also did their town proud. A large parcel of garments they had made was dispatched with the help of the mayoress. They had a local working party that, once a week, would make garments to send out to servicemen. As early as October 1914 they had completed 114 garments. The Mother's Union contributed 128 garments, the St Peter's Union 30 garments and they had received 100 gifts, the total amounting to 372.

The women of Ludlow had their work cut out with the many war charities that were set up across the nation but they didn't shy away from their new-found responsibilities. When it became apparent that there were not enough men left to work the farms, they threw themselves into that work as well. Training was provided by Harper Adams Agricultural College at Edgmond near Newport, Shropshire where the women were taught poultry-keeping and general farm work.

It wasn't just agriculture that the women of Ludlow engaged in. In April 1915 the Ludlow Guild of Toymakers, under the wing of Mrs O. Pitman, 8 High Street, Ludlow was working hard to fill the void left by the German toy-making industry (any imports from Germany were now out of the question). In fact, the industries and businesses of the nation were openly encouraged to steal business away from Germany and it was seen as the patriotic thing to do. At an exhibition held in London, the Guild sold many of their toys and had orders flooding in; they were certainly doing their best for the war effort.

Sadly, despite the war having some positive effects for women, it also caused great strain. With their men away for months on end and not knowing if they would ever come back, plus the strain of keeping their families going, financially and practically, the Great War was a very difficult time for many women. This pressure became too much for one officer's wife who committed suicide in June 1918. Susan Lambert Benson was just 36 years old and had two children aged 1 and 3 years. Already suffering from depression and having had a nervous breakdown the year before her death, she was found with a large stone tied around her neck at the bottom of a pond.

The women of Ludlow did a great deal of charity work during the course of the war and without their efforts it might have had a very different outcome. There was nothing that the womenfolk of Britain, Ludlow included, would not do to serve their king and country. Although there were many people in Ludlow and the surrounding area who willingly carried out their patriotic duties, there were others less eager to do so as we will find out in the next chapter.

# Crime, Punishment and Tribunals

**Suspicion and Rumour**

Along with the war came an ideal opportunity for wheeling and dealing, stealing and flouting the rules. However, it wasn't just criminals that came under scrutiny of the law and the locals. Many Germans living and working in Great Britain were interned, whether or not they were suspected of committing crimes, under the Aliens Act. This Act restricted the movements of known aliens: those of foreign birth living and working in the UK. They were obliged to register and obtain permits if they wanted to travel a greater distance than 5 miles. During the Great War more than 32,000 aliens were interned, so concerned were the authorities about spies compromising the war effort. This led to some interesting and embarrassing incidents in Ludlow when mistaken identity and the supposedly suspicious actions of some townspeople and visitors led to police inquiries and mild panic regarding completely innocent people.

There had been reports of a man entering the garage on Corve Street with the intent of hiring a car. Nothing wrong in that you might think, but remember this was wartime and everyone was on their guard lest a German spy should appear among them and cause mischief. For some reason the garage owner became suspicious and decided to contact the police, telling them that he had a German at the garage and would keep him there until the police came. However, when they arrived and spoke with a rather 'excited' garage owner, they discovered that the 'German' in question had left the garage and absconded up the street. The police located him in a pub, whereupon he was recognized by one of the policemen as someone who lived along the racecourse and had only wanted to hire the car to take a friend home.

In another incident a man was seen making a drawing of the river and bridge at Ludford (adjacent to Ludlow) and the local scouts were on to him, watching him like hawks. It was eventually discovered that he was an accomplished artist from Liverpool who regularly visited the town.

Local businesses were also up before the court for not registering aliens. A local farmer and boarding-house owner was fined £1 5s costs for not registering a Dutch alien who had stayed at his boarding-house. He could have been given a six-month prison sentence or a £100 fine.

**Put That Light Out**

A great many regulations came into force as part of DORA. One of these was the enforcement of lighting restrictions. Homes and businesses had to either turn off or obscure their lights during certain hours of the night and it wasn't long before some of Ludlow's residents began to fall foul of the regulations and found themselves in court as a result.

Mr William C. Portlock, who managed a fruit shop in the Bull Ring, was charged with flouting the lighting restrictions by allowing light from his shop to be seen from across the street at 8.30pm on 1 April 1916 and he was fined 5s. Similarly, the manager of a cheese and bacon shop in the High Street was fined 5s for also failing to obscure the light in his shop. They weren't the last, either. A butcher in Tower Street was also fined. In one week alone there were five such breaches of the lighting order and there was no leniency in any of these cases. All the culprits were fined. Failure to adhere to DORA restrictions was taken very seriously indeed and seen as an offence against national security. In order to help locals remember the lighting curfew, the local church – St Laurence's – became involved by agreeing to ring the church bells five minutes before the curfew came into force.

**Neighbour Disputes**

One interesting case that appeared in court in August 1916 involved a corporal with thirteen children. Two of his children, aged 12 and 15, were on remand from the workhouse having been charged with stealing food from a neighbouring house. However, the father was less than sympathetic to the householder, stating that the woman shouldn't have left her door open.

Of the thirteen children, the eldest boy had been killed in action but there were still eight others living at home. Their mother was struggling to manage on the separation allowance, and with the price of food going up the children often went hungry. The court decided that the 15-year-old would be sent to a home for two years, for which his father would pay from his army allowance. The 12-year-old was bound over on a good behaviour bond for a year. Even the children of soldiers at war could not get away with their misdemeanours.

**Fighting Germans, Austrians and Drink**
Considering the bleakness of war and accompanying financial hardships, it was no wonder that many people turned to drink. The courts were full of men and some women who were charged with being drunk and disorderly, often resulting in violence or damage to property. Drunk and disorderly behaviour was a problem that irked those who favoured temperance and abstinence during wartime. There were often comments in the local press from people who were disgusted by those unable to control their alcohol addiction when there were men risking their lives abroad that either weren't allowed or didn't have time to drink.

Alcohol consumption was becoming a real problem in Britain. In 1914 there were around 184,000 convictions for drunkenness. This fell to around 84,000 in 1916 and again to around 29,000 in 1918. The government and military authorities were concerned that excessive drinking was adversely affecting the war effort, and to counteract this they had reduced public house opening hours. Changes were also made in beer production, making it a weaker brew.

On some occasions men who had fought in the war but been invalided out or were home on leave found themselves before the courts for being drunk. The judge was often, but not always, more lenient with them. One man – discharged wounded soldier George Wilkes of Lower Galdeford, Ludlow who had been before the court previously on similar charges – was charged with being drunk and disorderly in the Bull Ring, Ludlow in December 1916. It was noted in court that everything possible had already been done to help him, but as soon as he drew his pension he spent it on drink. It was the opinion of the arresting policeman that Mr Wilkes thought everyone in the town looked down on him and he had nowhere to live.

The mayor, presiding, was lenient on account of his war wounds and fined him 5s with a warning that if he was seen in court again he would be imprisoned. Unfortunately that warning went unheeded and Wilkes was once more in court in January 1917, this time being found drunk and disorderly in Tower Street, Ludlow. As he was trying to sort himself out and was due to be married soon, his case was adjourned for two months.

This case wasn't over just yet but it does have a happy ending. Mr Wilkes was brought before the court again in March 1917 when it was learned that he had behaved himself and no further complaints had been made against him. The case was adjourned for another month. When that month was up there were no complaints reported and the case was dismissed, to which Mr Wilkes said: 'Thank you, Sir.'

**Prisoners of War**
There had been much talk about German prisoners of war being housed in Ludlow and employed to work on the farms. By the end of March 1918 a group of them were living at the racecourse and were working at Ludford Park and a few farms in the area. Around forty of them were expected at the Race Club Stables near the station. The news was described as an 'interesting event in the history of Ludlow of the Parish'. It was hoped that they were going to help cultivate the racecourse, or the Old Field as it was also known, for extra vegetable production.

Prisoners of war were a useful propaganda tool. How a country treated its captives was scrutinized and each was keen to show how well they looked after them as this would appear to give them the upper hand. Both sides claimed that their prisoners were ill-treated. It is estimated that between 8 and 9 million men were taken captive during the war.

**The Trouble with Tribunals**
Soon the courts would be turning their attentions to tribunals where

# DISCOVER MORE ABOUT MILITARY HISTORY

**Pen & Sword Books** have over 4000 books currently available, our imprints include; Aviation, Naval, Military, Archaeology, Transport, Frontline, Seaforth and the Battleground series, and we cover all periods of history on land, sea and air.

Keep up to date with our new releases by completing and returning the form below (no stamp required if posting in the UK).

Alternatively, if you have access to the internet, please complete your details online via our website at **www.pen-and-sword.co.uk.**

**All those subscribing to our mailing list via our website will receive a free e-book,** *Mosquito Missions* by Martin W Bowman. Please enter code number ACC1 when subscribing to receive your free e-book.

Mr/Mrs/Ms .................................................................................................................

Address .......................................................................................................................

....................................................................................................................................

Postcode................................... Email address.....................................................

Website: www.pen-and-sword.co.uk  Email: enquiries@pen-and-sword.co.uk
Telephone: 01226 734555   Fax: 01226 734438
Stay in touch: facebook.com/penandswordbooks or follow us on Twitter @penswordbooks

Freepost Plus RTKE-RGRJ-KTTX
Pen & Sword Books Ltd
47 Church Street
BARNSLEY
S70 2AS

applicants could appeal against being called up and attempt to gain some level of exemption. Tribunals were often disorganized, inconsistent and contradictory, leaving many confused and angry at the outcomes. Unfortunately, appeals were no better. Tribunals took place regularly in Ludlow, both borough and rural. Mayor Valentine and G. Randles – the latter was to lose a son in the war himself – were present at the borough tribunals.

 In the early days of the tribunals the press were prohibited from entering but this soon changed when a level of transparency was demanded. On one occasion, of the thirteen cases heard two were adjourned, seven postponed, three refused and only one received an absolute exemption. The exemption was granted to the son of a man whose other two sons were already serving in the army.

One of the claims refused was from a bricklayer's labourer. He was the eldest of four sons. One brother was already at the front and another in training, while the third's group was about to be called up. The applicant wanted to stay at home to care for his mother.

Another interesting case to come before the tribunals was that of a stone company and a quarryman. The company had applied for all of its twenty-two workers to be exempted. They could not replace these skilled men, despite every effort to do so. Because working at the quarry face was dangerous, they couldn't get married men to replace those who were eligible for service and it was hard to persuade younger men to work there for the same reason. The company had been supplying stone for military road-making and 30 per cent of their workforce had already enlisted. They had lost some business in 1914 due to a reduction in the workforce, with a further 17 per cent loss of men in 1915. Although an exemption was granted, there was much debate and confusion about the decision. 'It seems very unsatisfactory. We don't know whether we must get men or stone,' was the chairman of the tribunal's remark.

As the death toll continued to rise sharply, a revised list of reserved occupations was introduced. This would see a flood of appeals and applications, often overwhelming the tribunals. Exemptions were becoming more and more limited to men of responsibility and experience in firms – e.g. managers, etc. – and to married men over the age of 30. All single men who had not already been called up soon would be.

Disagreements and controversy were commonplace at these tribunals. One particular protest that came from the Shrewsbury Advisory Committee was regarding the appointment of paid military officers from the army representing the chief recruiting officer at appeals tribunals. Lord Derby himself replied, stating that the appointment was more economical and efficient, but it remained an unpopular decision.

So concerned was the War Office about the state of some tribunals and how they were managed, especially the conduct of some of the military representatives, that they made the bold statement that they were 'battling with stupidity' because the representatives did not always follow War Office instructions.

Statistics published in the 11 March issue of the *LA* showed that from 70 cases and 6.25 hours of sitting time, the Ludlow Rural District Tribunal had granted 21 postponements for 6 months, 1 postponement for 4 months, 14 postponements for 3 months, 7 postponements for 2 months, 12 postponements for 1 month and 1 postponement for 14 days; in addition, 8 were refused, 5 were adjourned and 1 was out of date.

It was noted that as the war went on, a greater number of applications for exemptions were coming from farmers for their farm hands, the numbers of which were being badly depleted by enlistment. So incensed were some of the locals about the tribunals that they started writing letters to the local paper:

> Knowing the County's need for men and to assist Mr Asquith and Lord Derby in their pledge of single men first, I hope our Town Council will loyally set the example to other employers of labour by liberating all single men of military age in the employment of the corporation, employing married men in their stead.

Complaints didn't just come from the locals who weren't eligible for military service, but also from some of those attested men. The following letter from such a married man was complaining about how the tribunals were conducted. He was not at all happy about the stone company case mentioned above:

If an employer sat on the tribunal whilst exemptions were being claimed for some of his workmen and they were granted same or postponement my contention is that it is not valid and should be cancelled as influence would have such a bearing on the application. Do they expect married men to go whilst these strong and healthy young men are exempted?

It wasn't just the local civilians who were breaking the law or trying to gain exemption from being called up. In one case soldier John Cadwallader from Cainham of the 3/1 Shropshire Yeomanry was charged with absenteeism from his regiment in Wrexham. He was arrested the day after he had received his call-up papers and was remanded to await military escort.

It was easy, in the heat of war and the need for patriotism, for people to think that those brave men who volunteered to fight for king and country were the epitome of heroism and righteousness. However, as in any occupation or walk of life, the war years were subject to abuse by opportunist criminals.

In 1918 a soldier aged 27 was accused of stealing a gold watch, brooch and a lamp. He had allegedly broken into houses at Clee Hill and Tenbury and was no stranger to being light-fingered, having also been convicted of petty crimes back in 1912.

In between these offences, he had been fighting in France and Belgium, having enlisted in September 1914. He was wounded in May 1915 and invalided back to the UK. When he recovered he went to Gallipoli but was again sent back to the UK after contracting dysentery in September 1915. He had been declared a deserter in September 1917 and there were also some discrepancies regarding his war honours.

Descriptions of this man prior to his enlistment were not encouraging. He was described by the local press as 'a waster' but, perhaps surprisingly, initially proved to be a good soldier with no issues. Perhaps his experiences of war had scarred him in more ways than the courts or his military superiors realized. For his later offences he received a twelve-month prison sentence with hard labour. It obviously wasn't easy for every serviceman to adjust back to civilian life.

There was much confusion and disagreement within the tribunals about how to handle conscientious objectors. The validity of their claims of not wanting to fight for moral or religious reasons was subject to rigorous questioning and they were treated with suspicion. It wasn't beyond the imagination of some local men to claim to have 'seen the light' just to avoid military service.

In the Ludlow Borough Tribunal in September 1916 a painter and decorator who was a member of the Christadelphian Body had replied to a letter previously sent by the tribunal regarding the nature of his work and he said he was working at a timber yard. However, the tribunal thought he was working in munitions away from Ludlow. The reasoning was to ensure that just as servicemen were away from their homes and families, conscientious objectors should be too.

The tribunals were also despairing of 'single shirkers' and moved to not hear any further cases regarding married men until all the cases relating to single men had been heard. However, the ensuing vote was a tie, so things remained as they were for the time being.

An interesting case to come before Ludlow Borough Tribunal was that of the owner of the Picture House. In an age before television and the internet, the only way people could get news was via the newspapers or the cinema. The Picture House had been showing patriotic films and footage from the battlefields as well as light entertainment films, thereby fulfilling its role of simultaneously providing information and entertainment. The 40-year-old owner was married with two children and had been classified as class A. His argument for exemption was that if the Picture House was left to anyone else to manage, it could be dangerous to the public.

Mr Randles, who had lost his son in the war, suggested that the owner be made to use some of his time doing work of national importance as the Picture House was not in operation all the time. The secretary replied that the man had volunteered two afternoons a week to dig gardens for the Food Production Committee. However, the tribunal was not satisfied with this, claiming that he should dig for twice as long. The reply was that if he did so, he would have to sell up as he also had his own large garden to dig and was often tired after a stint in the Picture House. The tribunal was unmoved, stating that everyone had to make sacrifices. Their compromise decision was that while the owner was engaged in his present occupation he wouldn't be called up as long as he did work of national importance for the equivalent of two days a week.

By October 1917, it was suggested that single class A men should enlist from the munition works and the whole issue of recruitment was under scrutiny. The Ludlow Borough Tribunal was keen to follow this resolution as they were anxious to be seen to be doing their utmost to get men to enlist. They were aware that there were many eligible men in the town who had not enlisted and they regarded this as a mark of shame on the town.

It seems incredible that despite the fact that the country was engaged in the most major conflict in history, opportunist criminals were not deterred from operating. What they hadn't taken into account, however, was the patriotism and sense of justice employed by the local courts and miscreants were often dealt with severely. After all, there was a world war in progress and anyone who was not toeing the line and doing their duty was looked down on and treated accordingly.

# CHAPTER 8

# Letters Home

It was a terrible shock for many of the young lads when they engaged in battle for the first time. Previously most of them had probably not ventured much further than the next nearest town or city, and although the recruitment campaigns appealed to their patriotic side and were heavy on urging them to do their duty, the theory and reality were very different.

One day they had been farming the fields or serving customers in a shop and the next they were transported to barracks and beginning training. The novelty of the situation and the camaraderie of 'all lads together' soon wore off once they were being blasted by shells and fired at by German machine guns. Often the only comfort to be had was a letter from home and the soldiers from Ludlow certainly enjoyed putting pen to paper when they could.

## Don't Worry About Me

The local newspapers and parish magazines carried such letters in their pages and, despite censorship, gave an interesting insight into real military life from training to the trenches and at sea. Some of the letters were stark and to the point, leaving no illusions as to the brutality and terror of war as shown by this extract from a letter sent to Mr J. Diggle, headmaster of the local National School, from an ex-pupil of his, Sergeant Charles Francis, 1st Battalion KSLI who lived at 41 Upper Galdeford, Ludlow:

> It is terrible where we are at present as there are so many unburied bodies and the stench is almost unbearable in this hot

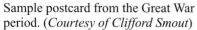

A MESSAGE.

If our feeling run down,
Now Matches cost double,
You'll soon wear a smile,
That extinguishes trouble,
By coming down here,
To have a good cuddle.

I miss you so, my loved one,
Now we are far apart,
For tender thoughts arise dear,
Within my loving heart.

EVER IN MY THOUGHTS

Sample postcard from the Great War period. (*Courtesy of Clifford Smout*)

Another Great War postcard. (*Courtesy of Clifford Smout*)

weather … The stench is almost more than one can stand and plenty of dead horses lie about unburied. There are also hundreds of bodies barely covered by the soil so the earlier we move along the better for our health for the country all round is just one large burial ground.

The realization that at any moment they might become one of the many wounded or dead must have been difficult to endure. However, the letters home also spoke of hope and of a life serving their king and country that 'was not too bad': '… arrived quite safe. Slept on bricks last night, one blanket. I think I embark today. Will write later. Plenty of fun here. Life too good.'

Whereas some men resigned themselves to the fact that they were in a place that could only be described as hell and resolved to make the best of it, others found the experience overwhelming and didn't hold back from telling their families and friends back home how they felt, as stated in this extract from a letter sent from Boulogne, France on 15 August 1914:

> Just arrived in France more dead than alive after being packed like sardines in a troopship. We begin a hundred mile march tomorrow for the Belgian frontier and work our way into Germany.
>
> Harold Kershaw, RAMC.

Letters were also sent regularly by some servicemen from the Ludlow Territorials, G Company, entitled 'Doings of the Ludlow Territorials from their training camp in South Wales'. The camaraderie was particularly striking:

> On the march the company is readily picked out by its swinging stride, the singing of one of the popular choruses of some new song, and the jokes they crack at the expense of one of their chums who has had the misfortune to meet with a blistered foot, or some other temporary calamity.

This was while the company was guarding Barry Docks and forts at Barry Island and Lavennoch, Wales. It was reported that aliens were a real risk and were often caught 'prowling around' by the company. So, even in training and in guarding the home front, life was neither dull nor without risk.

## Post

One soldier, not wishing to rely on posting his mail through the official channels for fear of it getting lost, was Harold Kershaw who enlisted the help of a woman he met on a train to deliver his post. He met Lydia Holland, who was returning home from France, in Amiens where she

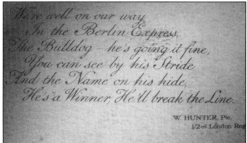

We're well on our way
In the Berlin Express,
The Bulldog – he's going it fine,
You can see by his Stride
And the Name on his hide,
He's a Winner, He'll break the Line.

W. HUNTER. Pte.
1/2nd London Regt

Great War Christmas cards. (*Courtesy of David Phillips*)

With
Best Wishes
for
A Happy Christmas
from
The Officers, Warrant Officers,
Non-Commissioned Officers and Men.

VI DIVISION
BRITISH EXPEDITIONARY FORCE
1915.

saw some British soldiers on the next line, one of whom was Harold. She offered to post his letters for him and he agreed. Lydia wrote a note accompanying Harold's letters to his parents stating how anxious he knew they were about them, but she reassured them that 'he seemed quite alright and very cheerful.'

## Best Days of our Lives

Another headmaster, Mr J. Barker of the British Schools, also received regular letters from his ex-pupils who had enlisted. In one from 9805 Corporal George Rogers, B Company, 1st KSLI, 16th Brigade, 6th

Division, there is some interesting insight into a soldier's daily life and how important the memories of his time at school were to him:

> … though years are past since I last sat at the old desk and many miles separate us I still think of happy times spent there … we have been having some awfully wet weather out here of late which has made the trenches very bad, being up to one's knees in mud.
>
> We are at present billeted in a large factory having been relieved from the trenches for a few days' rest. Those at home can hardly imagine what a relief it is to us, for it tells on one's nerves watching and fighting day after day and night after night, but we are still merry and bright under the circumstances, for we have come out here to win, and win we mean to.

One lucky sailor who took part in the Great Sea Battle – the Battle of the North Sea on 24 January 1915 – regaled the local people through the pages of the *Ludlow Advertiser* about his exploits that day:

> We took the great part of sinking a ship and also damaging one of three destroyers. It was a bit of a rough time as we did not know any minute that some of us would be killed … It was a sight to see, but I hope and trust that the next time we take part that we shall make them pay for it dear.
>
> I don't suppose they will want to come over to the East Coast again killing the women and children. You see they met men this time, not babies.

Able Seaman G. Fox was aboard the HMS *Aurora* during this battle (also known as the Battle of Dogger Bank). The *Aurora* was an *Arethusa*-class vessel and luckily suffered only minor damage when she was struck three times during the battle.

Another letter, from a soldier this time, gave some indication as to the conditions of his accommodation: 'When we are relieved from the trenches, we live in "dugouts". These "dugouts" are not like those described in the trenches. I had to turn contortionist the last one I was in.'

Life in the trenches was not only hazardous but devoid of any home comforts the lads might have been used to. Here in another letter dated

Some Great War postcards made fun of the Germans. (*Courtesy of Clifford Smout*)

16 March received by the headmaster Mr Diggle, brothers E. Bishop, T.H. Bishop and W. Bishop of the 1st Monmouthshire Regiment, D Company, 43rd Platoon who were at the front in France saw action many times and were only too aware of the risks involved, particularly following this unfortunate incident:

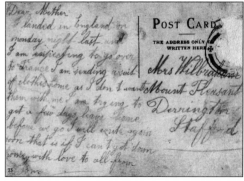

Great War postcards. (*Courtesy of Clifford Smout*)

As I write this a Jack Johnson landed about 30 yards from here (eh, what!) … Today I saw a Jack Johnson knock a church to smithereens. The town here is all in ruins, but the Germans are paying for it dearly … Our password here is 'keep your napper down', and you have to here, I can tell you.

A 'Jack Johnson' was a slang term used by the soldiers for a heavy 15cm German shell when it impacted the ground and exploded in a distinctive black cloud of dust. It was named after the Texan World Heavyweight Boxing Champion of the time, giving some idea of its power.

It may have been monotonous for some in the trenches, the tedium only interspersed with shelling and fighting, so letters from home would have provided a welcome respite. However, the war soon began to be fought from the air as well as the ground and this account by Lance Corporal J. Woodhouse, also an ex-pupil of Mr Diggle, tells of a breathtaking aerial battle played out above the trenches:

> We are having glorious weather now, so you can guess we have plenty of aeroplanes up now. They are breaking the monotony of the trench warfare too … We witnessed a very exciting battle in which there were about 7 or 8 planes taking part. The majority were German … (You will understand the sky was full of twisting shells from aircraft guns) when we noticed a shell burst in the tail of a German machine. It at once turned and dived sharply towards the earth, but somehow the aviator managed to volplane safely to the ground.

For many of the men, it wasn't the shell fire, machine guns or gas that accounted for them but the many illnesses such as typhoid and gastritis that became – unsurprisingly considering the squalid state of the trenches – rife among the servicemen:

> I am in one of the many hospitals out here with gastritis … I shall never forget my first experience of going into action. On the night of June 15th the battalion marched to within two miles of the firing line just beyond _____, and dug ourselves in under the railway, this to be a cover against the enemy's aircraft passing over … We had not gone far before we were met with a terrible hail of shells from the enemy's artillery … Once, and only a night or two before I came here, a bullet grazed my shoulder and went through a sandbag which one of my comrades was carrying. But all these little things come in a soldier's life.

The letters sent by those fighting in the war were also used to the advantage of the recruitment drive, although from the descriptions of the negative events as detailed in some letters one has to wonder whether this actually deterred more potential volunteers than it enticed:

> I know there are thousands of men in England at the present time who in peace time love to play football and other such games,

and to be called sportsmen; why don't they prove it by joining the Army or Navy, and take part in the biggest game the world has ever known?

Lance Corporal J. Woodhouse, 1st KSLI. August 20th 1915.

Presumably some men did not enlist because they didn't want to get blown up by a shell or had what they felt were more pressing concerns at home. Still, those who were fighting retained a sense of humour to get themselves through the nightmare of the conflict, as Drummer W. Wingate, 10(s) Battalion, Royal Warwickshire Regiment, shows here:

> They [the Germans] are very annoying when they start shelling, for they wait till meal-times and when we get our food nicely cooked and over come a few shrapnel shells, followed by a few rifle grenades. I don't know whether it is the flavour of the bacon or whatever we are cooking that tempts them or the smoke from the fire …

Of course, those engaged in warfare were not always fighting. Some were there to look after the wounded, such as Percy Cash, RAMC who was working on board a hospital ship after having made a delivery of medical supplies in the area of Malta. He wrote to Mr Diggle on 20 August 1915:

> The next step was to prepare beds for recovering the wounded from the various boats which were bringing the case direct from _____ a few miles away. For a whole week the strength and courage of our Corps was tried to the utmost. Quite 1,400 wounded were accommodated including 67 Officers, some badly wounded. One Officer had his right leg blown off … On the voyage home we buried 28, the low percentage speaks for itself, and proves beyond doubt the work carried out by doctors, nurses and the R.A.M.C.

**Captured**

Unfortunately, some of those serving abroad found themselves as prisoners of war, as was Private J.E. Bishop of the 3rd Monmouthshire Regiment. He was in a concentration camp or *Gefangenenlager* in

Stendal, Germany with around 6,000 other prisoners: French, English, Belgian and Russian soldiers. In a letter he told of his daily routine there: 'The camp here is kept very clean, as the barracks. There is a lovely swimming bath, we have been using nearly every day, but the water is getting cold so it is has been arranged for us all to have a hot spray bath which is a treat.'

Private Bishop also went on to describe the entertainment they made for themselves by way of a concert between all the different prisoners. He noted the Russians' talent for dancing and the French prisoners' singing ability.

The servicemen used letters home to request certain items such as mouth-organs, footballs and boxing gloves, and as a conduit to pass on their thanks to the people of Ludlow for sending parcels of food. Sometimes tips were given on which food items to avoid; in Private Bishop's case this was bread as it went 'bad' before reaching him. He preferred Quaker oats biscuits instead.

It is clear that the letters exchanged between family and friends that were often published in local newspapers or parish magazines were a vital lifeline between the soldiers at war and those left behind at home. When it is considered that in any given week of the war the postal service was delivering around 12 million letters, postcards and parcels to and from the worst war zones the world had ever seen, not to mention soldiers being moved around at a moment's notice, it's remarkable that any post reached its recipients at all.

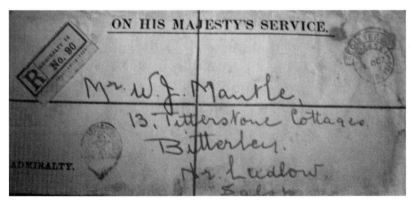

Envelope from a letter sent from the navy during the Great War. (*Courtesy of Margory Sheldon*)

# CHAPTER 9

# Livid from Ludlow and the Role of the Newspapers

If you want a snapshot of the strength of feeling in any given era, reading the correspondence pages of the local press would be a good start. The *LA* gives an interesting insight into the events and issues that concerned the townsfolk around that time.

**Read All About It**

One of the first concerns voiced by Ludlow residents and readers of the newspaper was the hoarding of food and the hiking of prices, as this concerned gentleman warned against:

> I respectfully but firmly appeal to my fellow townsmen, especially the more well-to-do classes, not to lay up stores of foodstuffs, or articles of consumption as any such action must tend to raise prices against the poorer classes and put it out of their power to obtain the necessities of life …

The poor of Ludlow were catered for by the Workhouse Union but the added pressures of wartime and potential impending shortage of food and resources, along with charity work being needed to support those at war and refugees, meant there was undue strain on the already scarce finances available.

In these days of national distress it is hoped that all class feeling will disappear, but this cannot be the case if poorer classes feel they have a grievance against their better off brethren. It is our duty as Englishmen to share a common lot and sink or swim together.

Henry Thomas Wayman, Aug 7th 1914

**Not Playing Ball**

However, it appeared that not everyone was playing ball, as was pointed out in a letter written by the Reverend A.E. Stewart-Scott of Downton Vicarage, Ludlow. He was outraged by the 'deplorable' actions of some customers and tradesmen in the town who he accused of 'profiteering'. He had one thing to say to them: 'God takes care of number one, and the devil takes the hindermost.'

During this time of great stress and uncertainty, the majority of townspeople in Ludlow were fiercely patriotic and frequently took umbrage at those who they saw as shirking their responsibilities and thereby potentially helping the enemy to win the war:

> Would it not be possible to present the white feather to all the young men who do not offer their services at their country's call? What cowards the young men must be who play cricket and other games when England needs them.
> One of the girls, Ludford, Ludlow, September 5th 1914.

Although many people shared the sentiment, some were outraged that a 'mere girl' would dare to question who volunteered to fight and who did not. However, the girls were not to be outdone and, egged on by the offence they seemed to have caused, they kept writing in support of the white feather comment:

> In this case the cap fits. Instead of wearing it he rushes into abuse and hides himself behind the shield (medically unfit)… From information received (I quote his words) when he tried to enlist in the Army the doctor passed him, except for his teeth, but since the teeth order has been cancelled, he has kept in the background behind the shield of medically unfit. The white feather is a suitable emblem for such so-called men.
>
> Another of the girls, October 3rd 1914.

The boys were incensed and accused the girls of writing on a subject they knew little about:

> I might suggest that she is suffering (like the Kaiser) from delusion, probably brought on by a nightmare…
> One of the boys, October 1914.

Another issue on the minds of the townspeople was the playing of sport during wartime or, more precisely, why seemingly able-bodied and fit young men were still out on the sports fields rather than presenting themselves for enlistment.

The Reverend L.R.C. Baggot from Stanton Lacy had previously given his scathing opinion on this matter, particularly with regard to football, and in reply the 'Old 'Un' [pseudonym of Mr Brown, see below] said:

> I myself see no harm in games or sports during war time. We can't all join the army and recreation is good for all of us.
> September 26th 1914.

The Old 'Un went on to accuse the Reverend of enjoying his fishing and shooting, said that it seemed to be one rule for the rich and one rule for the poor and suggested the closure of the picture houses and inns as well. This appears to have riled the Reverend even more, as his reply to the Old 'Un states:

> Mr Brown seems to think that I disapprove of football as a game. He is quite wrong. In my younger days I played a good deal myself. In my older I have always encouraged it as my Stanton Lacy boys can witness. But what I do say is that this is not the time for football or any games.
> September 19th 1914.

**Lifeline**

As well as offering an insight into people's feelings on the issues surrounding the war and local life, the newspapers also provided a much-needed lifeline and means of communication. They gave reports on what was happening in the war, as well as essential information from the government on new laws that were being passed and also the people's responsibilities as British subjects in aiding the war effort. In addition, news of the local lads who had been wounded, killed, were missing or had been taken prisoners of war could be seen within their pages.

However, it wasn't just the rights and wrongs of who did or didn't fight or the price of food that concerned people. There were also worries about the lack of material for clothing civilians:

> At this present moment all our thoughts are turned, and quite rightly so, on the equipment of the Navy and Army, but what we are apt to forget is that warehouses and shops must be stocked before they can supply their customers.
> M.A. Williams, Feb. 1915

The writer thought that there should be a return to the teaching of traditional skills such as weaving and spinning that had been handed down over hundreds of years from generation to generation. It was thought that if Great Britain could once again become self-sufficient instead of relying on imports, this would greatly help the war effort and the country's economy; they could also steal trade from Germany.

The *LA* also made comments on various subjects that affected the town. One such comment dealt with people doing their bit but that in some quarters this was being taken quite so far. In particular the paper was referring to veterans training to be the Home Guard:

> There is pathos as well as comedy in the sight of a bevy of 'veterans' drilling with dogged perseverance, sans uniform, sans rifle, sans everything except enthusiasm. If they may never be called up to defend us, they deserve commendation for trying to qualify for the task, and, what is infinitely harder, for enduring ridicule instead of the praise they should receive. (*LA*, 20 March 1915)

**Women's Work?**

When it became apparent that the country was going to have to find many more men to fight and the question arose of women taking the place of men, where possible, in the jobs they had temporarily vacated, not everyone was sure about the wisdom of women leaving the home and their traditional roles.

Three Ludlow ladies who answered the call for women volunteers to go and work at Vickers' Works munitions factory in Washwood Heath, Birmingham at the end of December 1915 appear to have been ridiculed by other women for doing so:

> When we left Ludlow, we were laughed and jeered at by other girls, and told, amongst other things, that we were going to work for nothing; others said that we were going for our own pleasure, etc. We wish to say to the numerous girls in Ludlow who at this time of national crisis are simply idling their time in doing nothing that we are quite satisfied with the work we have to do; that the wages are good; and we have found good lodgings; and that moreover we are possessed of a clear conscience in the fact that we are doing our bit for our King and country.

However, the following writer was not exactly sympathetic to the munitions girls' plight:

> At the present critical time of our country's welfare we are asked to economise. Is it economy for girls to leave a good berth and home to go and work 11 hours a day for say 14s to 16s per week, which to say the least does not do a girl brought up in Ludlow any physical good …
> One who knows Ludlow and Birmingham.

Yet another reader, T. Harcourt Llewellyn of Birmingham, thought that even though Ludlow women 'tend to have a dreamy, faraway look' in their eyes that they most definitely were not shirkers.

**The Lighter Side of Life**
The newspapers would often also carry funny cartoons to present a lighter side to the war, either poking fun at the German troops or the new laws that had come into force. One particular cartoon shows the scene of a butcher's shop with the butcher warning a local man against loitering outside his shop. The caption reads: 'You bustle along now!

If you let one of these 'ere Zeppelin crews so much as catch a sight of our lovely sausages, my lad, we're done for!'

Some readers were incensed about all the frivolity and entertainments going on in the town. This particular reader was not happy about the Picture House in Ludlow showing films: 'I could not bring myself to spend money on amusements which might be better spent in helping to alleviate the sufferings of our boys at the front, or in hospital, or elsewhere.'

However, even the newspapers themselves were not above the effects of hardship as the war progressed. Soon paper itself became a scarce commodity and the papers were obliged to reduce content in a bid to conserve it. In fact, in November 1917 the *LA* apologized to its readers who weren't able to secure a copy due to the restriction on paper, which by then was down to 50 per cent of its pre-war usage.

The newspapers were the main source of information for people, alongside Lantern Lectures that popped up now and then. Such lectures were planned about the war and were to be organized by the War Savings Committee. One was entitled 'The War on the Land' and was read by the local rector. There were also lectures on self-sacrifice, denial and reducing waste. Another lecture asked: 'What is the Navy Doing?'

Even after the end of the war, readers still sent in letters to the *LA* regarding their displeasure about what was happening in Ludlow. One reader pointed out that there was a national programme for change and wondered if Ludlow Council would be honouring it. He was referring to the lack of lighting in parts of Ludlow and wondering why Ludlow hadn't yet followed other towns in returning its lighting to pre-war levels. He was particularly concerned about ex-servicemen or the disabled who were at risk of falling or colliding with things because they couldn't see them in the dark: 'Even in France we had more light. We certainly had the very doubtful pleasure of seeing Fritz's star shells go up.'

After the war had ended and censorship was relaxed, the *LA* published an interesting account from a Ludlow PoW who had returned home. Private J.E. Bishop of the Monmouthshire Regiment had worked for the South Wales Railway before being called up when war was declared. He became a PoW after being captured by the Germans at the Second Battle of Ypres.

While a PoW, he was put to work in a variety of settings including a pickle factory, salt mine, canal and farm. With food being scarce, he was very glad of the parcels received from Ludlow. One good thing to come out of his time as a PoW was that he had learned to speak fluent German.

However, an argument between himself and a guard over the times he should start work saw him start a prison sentence of thirteen months at Cologne. It wasn't until Cologne experienced an uprising that a mob crashed through the gates and set him free, along with the other PoWs there. He travelled to the border of Holland and then caught a train to Rotterdam and was ferried home.

Newspapers had a clear and important role to play during the war years, even if some of their information was out of date or inaccurate by the time it was printed. In the days before the internet and computers and with cinema still in its infancy, local newspapers were the only line of public communication open to most people.

The armed services abroad had their own newspaper, the *Wipers Times*, which took a satirical look at things in the war and was very popular. Its name was derived from Ypres, a town in France that was often the scene of horrendous battles. British soldiers had difficulty in pronouncing it, so it became known as 'Wipers' and the name was adopted by their newspaper. Although newspapers were the mainstay of communication, the church also produced magazines which will be discussed in the next chapter.

# CHAPTER 10

# The Role of Religion

*'Rejoice with those who do rejoice, and weep with those who weep.'*

Religion paid a big part in people's lives during the war. It had, according to some clergy, seen a decline in previous years and many in church authority saw the war as a way to bring those parishioners that had strayed back into the fold. To them, patriotism was next to godliness and it was every Christian's responsibility to do their duty for the war effort. However, in many churches the war had the opposite effect with more people shunning religion.

**Fighting the Good Fight**

Many denominations fully supported the war, seeing it as a just battle against the tyranny and barbarism of the enemy. They had no objections to the use of force to achieve these aims, but there were also religious groups and individuals who were opposed to the war and they declined to fight on religious or conscientious grounds.

Although some conscientious objectors were opposed to fighting, they often took non-combatant roles as clergy or medics based near the front lines and aboard medical ships. They tended to the sick and wounded through the RAMC. Others supported the war effort at home through fund-raising and other similar activities.

Reading the *Ludlow Rural Deanery Parish Magazine*s gives a flavour of how the church and its faithful parishioners helped the war effort from the conflict's shocking beginning through to the bitter end.

T. Price, printer, advert in church magazine. (*Courtesy of Chris Deaves*)

Micklewright's advert in church magazine. (*Courtesy of Chris Deaves*)

The magazine also ran several adverts that give some idea of the types of shops and businesses in the town around this time. Some of them even based their adverts around the war.

The editorial of the *Ludlow Parish Magazine* September 1914 issue thought that 'The most terrible struggle in all history had come like an unexpected thunderclap.' The magazine advised the people of Ludlow to be prepared for many soldiers and sailors to be wounded or killed, and for 'anxious days of waiting for news'. There was a feeling within its pages that the people of Ludlow would stay calm and do their duty 'with manly determination and stubborn endurance'.

As news of the war and its consequences began to sink in, some of the local church events were abandoned or postponed including Church Day and the Sunday School Festival and many church services were altered 'to meet the needs of the present time of anxiety and trouble.'

## Christian Concerns

The church became a whirlwind of activity with new committees and working parties being set up, presenting plenty of opportunities for all those wishing to help in any way they could. They warned against waste and emphasized the need for everyone to operate with the greatest of frugality and economy.

The moment war was declared, the Ludlow Company officers were called for duty; all the Church Lads' Brigade also volunteered and ended up as part of the defence force for the Birmingham Aqueduct. The war united the people of Ludlow, whether churchgoers or not.

List of Officers, N.C.O's and Lads of the Ludlow Company now serving with H.M. Forces.

| | |
|---|---|
| Downes, Surgeon-Lieut. ... | R.A.M.C. |
| Marston, Lieutenant ... | K.S.L.I. |
| Adams, A ... ... ... | Manchester Regt. |
| Badlan, H. ... .. ... | K.S.L.I. |
| Baker, L. ... ... ... | K.R.R. |
| Bright, G. W. ... ... | K.S.L.I. |
| Butters, H. J. ... ... | Lancs. Fusiliers. |
| Burton, W. ... ... ... | K.R.R. |
| Bradley, H. ... ... ... | R.A.M.C. |
| Collier, J. W. (Wounded) ... | Staffs. Regt. |

List of some of the Ludlow Company Lads serving in 1915, church magazine. (*Courtesy of Chris Deaves*)

The Girls' Friendly Society, founded in 1875, had a branch in Ludlow and was much engaged in the war effort. The aim of the society was to work with the ideals of Christian fellowship through prayer and action, which they certainly did in Ludlow. They held a meeting on 12

August 1914 to discuss how they might best help with the war effort. They also had lectures on the war, the proceeds of which went to the National Relief Fund. This fund had been set up by the Prince of Wales to aid soldiers, sailors and their dependants who suffered hardship as a result of the conflict.

The children of the Bromfield School have been very active workers on behalf of the War Relief Funds, which the following list of their collections will show:

|  | £ | s. | d. |
|---|---|---|---|
| Prince of Wales' Fund ... ... ... | 0 | 11 | 0 |
| Belgian Fund . . ... ... ... | 0 | 5 | 0 |
| Work for Women Fund ... ... ... | 0 | 6 | 0 |
| Grand Duke Michael's Fund ... ... | 0 | 5 | 0 |
| Red Cross Fund... ... ... ... | 0 | 2 | 6 |
| Children's Hut (Y.M.C.A.) ... ... | 0 | 5 | 0 |
| Empire Day Penny Fund .. ... | 0 | 7 | 0 |
| Sick and Wounded (Red Cross) ... | 0 | 3 | 0 |

Out of their School hours they have also knitted the following articles : Socks, 41 pairs ; Mufflers, 12 ; Mittens, 36 pairs, the wool being provided by Mr. Winder, Mrs. Barber and others.

Bromfield School war efforts, church magazine. (*Courtesy of Chris Deaves*)

The outbreak of war was not mentioned in *The Sign*, a Christian magazine to which Ludlow parishioners had access, as it had already gone to print at the time. However, in the October 1914 issue it was suggested that the magazine was not a newspaper and its readers would look elsewhere for news about the war. The purpose of the parish magazine was to share topics close to religion and for those who wished 'to be reminded of their heavenly citizenship', although they did hope that there would be 'solace' or 'encouragement' for those who had been affected by the war: 'The herbs we seek to heal our woe, familiar by our pathway grow.' They urged people, regardless of how they felt, to just get on with their work.

The majority of them did just that. The church had a big presence in the town with its various clubs and societies. These included the Women's Guild, Men's Guild, Church Lads' Brigade, Cadet Corps, Children's Guild and the Ladies' Missionary Association, all of which were involved in the war effort in one way or another.

Nationally, the church published a series of booklets regarding religion and the war. Some of the titles included *Our Duty at Home in Time of War*, *The War and Our Social Problems* and *The War and Conscience*. *The Sign* also featured various articles outlining the duty of Christians during wartime and what they were doing all around the country to support the war effort. One such article published in December 1914 was about church nursing and ambulance work, highlighting how they were trained in first aid alongside the Church Red Cross Brigade that was the 'making of young women and girls'. Their role was to enable women to be more useful at home and to their country, more 'sympathetic' to suffering and to become 'more truly followers of Christ'.

The Archbishop of Canterbury even supported Lord Kitchener's call for people to help regarding temperance for newly-trained soldiers. The church and Lord Kitchener were both aware that not all dangers to the soldier came from the battlefield. The 'demon drink' at home was a risk too. Everyone was encouraged to abstain from drinking alcohol in support of the soldiers and this also led to a change in the licensing laws.

Illustration in church magazine: clergy at the battlefield. (*Courtesy of Chris Deaves*)

The church also produced another booklet, *The Happy Warrior*, that was full of 'daily thoughts' for servicemen, including bible verses and poems. They marketed it as a 'vital link' between the serviceman and home that would make an 'ideal Christmas Gift'! It was priced at 2d for a hardback version and 6d in cloth.

Within *The Sign* was a regular section called 'Our Query Corner' in which readers could submit questions about whatever was puzzling them at the time. Naturally, one particular topic that cropped up regularly was the current conflict, and this particular question of December 1914 demonstrated the church's stance on how they justified war.

The reader was pointed towards the Christian Standard that could be found in the 'Sermon on the Mount'. Here, man has the power of life or death and evil is overruled by God. Referring to the Great War, *The Sign* said that servicemen were 'doing work which is a judgment for wrong'.

As the war continued and the death toll rose, *The Sign* of February 1916 in its 'Thoughts for Soldiers and Others' section was pondering: 'Where is God in the Battlefield?' The answer was provided by a soldier: 'Entering into this war is like entering some great cathedral full of God's presence, and prayer and of praise.'

The church also disputed allegations of cowardice and answered the question as to why members of the clergy were not enlisting. The Bishop of London was once again ready with his reply. There were at the time (1916), 1,300 army chaplains and 300 naval chaplains serving abroad who were risking their lives doing the important job of ministering to the servicemen. In fact, sixteen such men in both services had already been killed. It was not the case that the clergy did not go to war; they simply held non-combatant posts.

## St Laurence's Church

St Laurence's Church in Ludlow stands proud for all to see as they enter the town and the earliest written record of its existence cites 1199 as the year when a church called St Laurence's was rebuilt. Why it was rebuilt remains a mystery; however, the position occupied by the church had been a holy site since before Saxon times.

During the Great War the church was to come into its own, especially as the lists of those wounded and killed began to increase in number and parishioners turned to the church for solace and to pray for an end to the conflict. In a parish of around 6,000, Ludlow's losses had a great effect upon the community.

The Church Lads' Brigade in Ludlow was a fertile training ground for future soldiers, although they were too young at an average age of 17 in the early part of the war. They did not get off lightly when they did enlist either, as many of their past members had unfortunately succumbed to injury or death while on the battlefield. Reports of their previous members' deaths appeared in the church magazine, including Lance Corporal Baron who was killed in action and Private Nott who died of wounds in a hospital at Boulogne. The Church Lads' Brigade also won many decorations over the course of the war including 10 VCs, 33 Military Crosses and 5 Croix de Guerre.

The various working parties set up in and around Ludlow also made 'comforts' to send to the soldiers and sailors fighting abroad and also those in hospitals. It was reported in the parish magazine of January 1915 that the local communities had made 18 pairs of cuffs and mitts,

COMFORTS FOR THE TROOPS.—The Queen's appeal to women of the Empire.

The Queen has addressed the following appeal to the women of the Empire.

Buckingham Palace.

I desire to express my most grateful thanks for the loyal and untiring support accorded to my Guild during the months of stress through which we have been passing.

The response to my first appeal has exceeded all expectations, but we have not yet arrived at a moment for any relaxation of our efforts in this direction, especially as winter is approaching, and I appeal once more to the loyalty and love shown me by the women of the Empire with confidence that they will continue in the future the splendid and generous support which I have been accorded in the past.

If the provision of comforts necessary for the well-being of our gallant sailors and soldiers is to be continued through the coming winter our efforts from the Queen Mary's Needlework Guild must be redoubled.

MARY R.

Letter from Queen Mary printed in the church magazine asking for help. (*Courtesy of Chris Deaves*)

125 pocket handkerchiefs, 7 pairs of socks, 4 pairs of bedsocks, 17 scarves, 4 belts, 9 hot water bottle covers, 11 roller bandages and 12 pillows! That's some hard work.

However, the locals didn't confine themselves to just fund-raising and helping the war effort abroad. They also cared for those civilians in need in their town who were already poor before the war ever began. Many years prior to the war Miss Windsor Clive (of the Clive of India family) had given money for nursing cover for the district and the cottage hospital; however, that could only stretch so far until Colonel Clive himself pledged more money for a district nurse who was to live with the maternity nurses at 10 Mill Street.

In the editorial of the parish magazine of July 1915, it was recognized that everyone was calling for donations for the various war charities and it was hoped that the poor, homeless and disabled children of the parish were not being overlooked in the process.

There was also the Queen Mary's Needlework Guild, the Ludlow Branch of which was formed in August 1914. Mayoress Valentine was president and the guild was busy making comforts and garments for the servicemen. In total, by 1915 the guild had sent 1,942 garments and comforts and that was without counting the numerous bandages and swabs they also made and distributed.

In the editorial of the church magazine of April 1915, there was a warning to the women of Bromfield and Ludlow. The South Wales Mounted Rifles were due to camp on the Old Field, but they didn't want the women to 'lose their heads over the fact'. There were concerns that the women would 'ogle' the soldiers and they were warned that the 'best sort of soldier' would find that 'common': 'Bromfield will not be added to the list of places which have made themselves notorious by their want of good manners and unseemly ways.'

With the advent of conscription in 1916, the church forwarded lists of all clergy who would be eligible for service in some way. It was pleasing to note that a large proportion of the clergy in the diocese covering Ludlow had already volunteered for duty. They were taking their patriotic and Christian duty very seriously.

The wounded servicemen who were taken to recover and convalesce at Stokesay Court at nearby Onibury, which was partly turned into a VAD hospital, were given bibles that many of them cherished. They wrote back to the matron there, telling her of the comfort their Stokesay bible gave them; others even wrote to ask if one could be sent out to them.

## Feeling the Pinch

As the war progressed with no end in sight, the local church began to feel the pinch in May 1916 when there were fears that it was struggling to continue its work in the town. One of the reasons cited was that one of their ordained priests, Mr Edwards, had been allowed three months off to help build a YMCA hut in France. The church pondered whether a layman could not have done the task instead, as it meant that St John's would be without a morning service until his return.

Despite such issues, the church was already looking ahead to the Britain that would remain after the war was over: 'If the church is going to make her voice heard, if she is going to take the lead in the re-creation of England, she must act as one body; her sons and daughters must unite and cooperate.'

As 1917 dawned, the church wished to give a message of hope by expressing their view that the worst was over. However, with the introduction of conscription followed by rationing, they were far from being out of the woods yet. The church was also keen to protect its buildings from potential air-raids, and in March 1917 St Lawrence's church warden renewed the relevant insurance at a cost of £43 but asked for contributions to help cover this outlay.

Owing to the severe winter, dark streets made more so due to the Lighting Act and an epidemic of influenza, the congregations at most churches in the town had diminished, as had their regular donations to the church plate. Therefore the churches were finding things just as hard as everyone else.

The mood of 1917 can only be described as one of doom and gloom. The war had been dragging on for three years with the end nowhere in sight and the harvests had been below average, but the church remained a beacon of hope. They encouraged people not to waste food and resources. Waste was unpatriotic and un-Christian. Even the paper shortage affected the church, with many of the local parish magazines having to reduce their number of pages, reduce the frequency of publication or increase their prices.

The church helped the war effort both home and abroad in so many ways, including asking for donations to a Wartime Emergency Fund

Illustrations in church magazine: 'Over the top.' (*Courtesy of Chris Deaves*)

that was used to give grants to house those working in munition factories in hostels via the Girls' Friendly Society. They also sent parcels out to servicemen. In the autumn of 1916 the Parish of Diddlebury, a small village between Ludlow and Much Wenlock, spent £38 18s 7d on fifty-nine Christmas parcels.

Those from the church who were serving abroad also wrote back to let their fellow parishioners know of their activities. One of the Church Army hut superintendents said in such a letter about his camp

– one that they had captured from the Germans – that humanity was divided into two sections there: 'those who have been over the top, and those who have not.'

This particular superintendent continued: 'The wonder is that the men seem to thrive on it. Unwashed, unshaven, and sometimes soaked with rain for days together, they seem hardened to every condition of soil or weather.'

**Ludlow the Hosts**
In September 1917 Ludlow was invaded by a group of children from Birmingham who were on a trip courtesy of a Country Holiday Fund. Although many people of Ludlow would have been pleased, seeing this as part of the war effort and their Christian duty, not everyone was equally enamoured with the idea. There were concerns regarding the calibre of the children, how they had been chosen and whether they might be infectious or not. These people were not only worried about the state and behaviour of the children but also whether the homes they were going to were suitable and had been appropriately vetted: 'It is not fair to Ludlow to have unhealthy or infectious children dumped here, and also not fair to Birmingham parents to have their children associate with others who are not healthy.'

Another way in which the church supported the war was by encouraging people to buy war bonds. Just as war costs millions of lives, it also costs money, much of it needed in a regular stream. In order to help finance the Great War, the government issued war bonds that people could buy. These were marketed aggressively and patriotically. As soldiers and sailors were risking their lives and dying for their country, the least those at home could do – or those who could afford to – was to buy war bonds which would be repaid in the future.

One marketing ploy that helped to bring the necessity of their purchase home was what a soldier or sailor might say if war bonds were not bought and his family or friends were being extravagant and not heeding the warnings about waste. After all, this was not just a war between countries but a war on waste: 'While I was freezing and going through it you were having the time of your lives. What have you left for me?' The bonds were also said to be a safeguard against unemployment and would help those who required financial assistance after the war.

Church members also sent out parcels for Christmas, held sales, collected eggs for soldiers and sailors, made garments and various comforts for the troops. They held knitting and sewing parties, grand concerts and other such entertainments. If they were going to be raising money and there wasn't much in the way of cheer and optimism, the least they could do was have fun while fund-raising. There was nothing they weren't prepared to do for their king and country in order to defeat the enemy.

**Self-sacrifice**
They were even prepared to forgo some of their usual entertainments and events. This was not always due to the feeling that they shouldn't have fun while the country was in crisis and men were dying abroad: it was a question of frugality and economy and the new laws that had been passed, together with rationing. For example, in early 1918 the local church at Ashford Carbonell had to stop their morning weekday services as they didn't feel that it warranted the heating and lighting required: 'Self-sacrifice is the call of the hour, and all must abide by the Nation's Rule. SOS is the mariner's "call of distress". It is also the nation's warning. "Sacrifice or Suffer", "Save or Starve".'

There was a sense of wistfulness with this comment in the editorial of April 1918: 'Some of you are old enough to remember pre-war days, when we went to the theatre and enjoyed it without feeling we were doing something we ought not to do.'

In March 1918 the church also drew attention to the importance of keeping infants safe and healthy. There was to be a travelling Infant Welfare Exhibition in Ludlow Town Hall with talks on childcare available to mothers: 'We have probably all heard the statement, based on official statistics of infant mortality, that is safer to be a soldier in the trenches than to be a baby in England.'

The church also played its part in ensuring that certain DORA regulations were adhered to; particularly the lighting order when the church bells would be rung five minutes before it came into force each day. The bells were an ideal way of conveying the message as they were distinctive and could be heard for miles around.

However, on one occasion when the 'joy bells' were rung over the period of an hour in December 1917 to celebrate the success at

Cambrai, some of the people in Ludlow mistook this as a sign that the war was over. This misinterpretation was not welcomed by the authorities, who commented that DORA was very serious and those spreading false rumours should be prosecuted.

By the beginning of 1918, there was renewed hope that there would finally be 'honourable and abiding peace'. Little did they know that their prayers were soon to be answered. However, even after the war's end, their sacrifice and hard work would continue for many years to come.

# Charity Begins at Home

Well before the outbreak of the Great War, Ludlow already had its fair share of charitable causes. Most cities, towns and villages in Britain had a mix of wealthy and poor inhabitants and the government and local councils had done much to try to address the needs of the poor with the introduction of workhouses and the passing of the Poor Law Act. The latter saw groups called the guardians form committees to oversee the finances, maintenance and running of the workhouses alongside any out-relief to those who preferred not to enter the workhouse or were not yet eligible.

**The Workhouse**
It is hardly surprising that the poor did not want to enter the workhouse if they could possibly avoid it. Conditions inside were deliberately kept stark and basic and the rules and daily rota harsh in an attempt to discourage people from entering. It was often marginally better to stay out as there was a degree of social stigma attached to living there and it was generally regarded as a last resort.

Ludlow was no exception; the town had its own workhouse with a board of guardians. As was often the case, the same people's names would appear on the committees of various charitable concerns and the council, more often than not those from the more well-to-do quarters of the town.

Despite its reputation, the workhouse proved to be financially rewarding for the businesses of the town who were often commissioned to supply provisions such as fuel, bed linen, candles, bread and other foodstuffs. One meeting of the board of guardians in Ludlow in September 1914 showed that the amount spent on relief in the Ludlow and Clee Hill district for just one fortnight was £35 14s 8d. At that time there were 102 inmates of the workhouse and 96 vagrants had been received, although this was lower than the 181 they had accommodated in the previous year.

As the workhouse had many mouths to feed and bodies to wash and clothe, local tradesmen were asked to put forward tenders regarding providing their wares to the workhouse. Some such local traders were Mr W. Tay, butcher, The Narrows, who was able to sell them beef at 6½d per lb; Mr Chas Tudge, Riddings, who sold milk at 8¾d per gallon; and Mr G. Pardoe who sold house coal for £1 0s 9d per ton. These prices were set to rise as the war continued, essentials became scarce and the price of wheat went up. Running a workhouse was expensive enough in times of peace but their budgets would be stretched almost to breaking point in wartime, along with everyone else's.

## Losing the Breadwinner

When war was first declared, concerns immediately arose for the dependants of the men going away to fight. These men were often the sole breadwinner of the family, and without their income many families would not have the means to survive. Also if the man's home was tied to his job as many farmers' cottages were, there was a real risk of hundreds of families becoming destitute and finding themselves evicted from their homes. If a man was subsequently killed and didn't return home or was severely wounded and couldn't work, his family would clearly be at risk.

In Parliament this issue was discussed and it was pointed out that local authorities already had the power to provide for those dependants whose menfolk worked for the local authority. The government's first port of call, in an attempt to help those in distress and in need of relief, was to ask employers to give consideration to keeping their employees in work and not add to the unemployment figures.

Rowland Hunt, MP for Ludlow, was keen to get the best assistance for the wives and children and other dependants of those men volunteering to enlist alongside the regular soldiers and sailors. He wanted assurances that all families of those in active service should be given sufficient food and clothing and would not lose their homes. Mr Hunt felt that as the servicemen were prepared to sacrifice their lives for their country, the very least their country could do in return was to look after their families.

Mr Tennant, Under Secretary of State for War, was sympathetic to the plea and it was noted that the wives of all married servicemen would receive a separation allowance. This would go some way towards providing for those the men were leaving behind, and the soldiers and sailors themselves would also be paid.

Now, as never before, it was vitally important to keep industry and businesses going, particularly those that would aid the war effort both at home and abroad. The government suggested other forms of employment could be offered that would be economically and psychologically better than jumping straight into offering financial assistance.

Although Ludlow was good at looking after its poor – particularly through the churches in the area, the local dignitaries and the well-to-do – when the Great War broke out it soon became obvious that the already stretched purse strings were about to be stretched even further. Would this mean that the local poor people would begin to lose out to war effort fund-raising? Would people start to shift their charitable donations to the soldiers and sailors or would they divide their charity between helping the poor at home and the war effort abroad? As food prices increased, food and other commodities became scarce and rationing and other restrictions began to bite, the charities doubtless found themselves fighting for people's shillings.

**Charity for War**
The advent of war caused many problems for the people of Ludlow. Not only did they have their own poor to care for, they now had the added pressure of raising money for the war, and wars on this scale cost vast sums of money. What little money they had was being stretched further and further. Charity and relief of distress caused by the war went hand-in-hand with doing one's duty and demonstrating patriotism. Those who could not fight put in every possible effort through fund-raising, donating or making items towards the war effort. During the Great War period around 17,899 British war charities were set up.

**The Prince of Wales's National Fund**

The day after war was declared, the National Relief Fund was set up by the Prince of Wales. It was to be a central fund for which the whole country would collect money through fund-raising events, collections and donations at a local level which would then be transferred to the national fund. The prince himself issued a request to all the women of the land to help raise money for this new fund, which was designed to aid both the families of those fighting and the sailors and soldiers themselves.

The churches of Ludlow often donated the sum of their collection plates after services had taken place and in one particular week St Laurence's Church raised £24 9s 1d, St John's £5 16s 4d and St Leonard's £1 14s 2d. These were not insignificant amounts for that particular era when it is considered how stretched people's finances already were.

Shropshire was also a leader when it came to looking after members of its own community who would be in need of relief once their menfolk went to war, with the formation of a Territorial Relief Fund.

Many reforms were also expedited in the face of the war, including the formation of a Ministry of Labour in 1916 and a Ministry of Health in 1919. In the years before the start of the war, nationally there were more than 300,000 applicants for relief but by 1922 this figure had risen to 2,000,000 despite government intervention and unemployment insurance.

Princess Mary, the king's 17-year-old daughter, decided she would also like to do her bit towards making life a little more comfortable for the fighting men. She sent out specially-designed brass boxes to

Princess Mary's Christmas box. (*Courtesy of Malcolm Williams*)

soldiers and sailors serving abroad, with each box containing her photograph, a writing set with a pencil in the shape of a bullet, cigarettes, lighter, pipe and pipe tobacco or sweets for non-smokers and a Christmas card. At Christmas 1914 426,724 of these boxes were sent out.

### The Belgian Refugees
When the government announced its plans to help the thousands of Belgian refugees who had been forced to flee their homeland by German troops, Ludlow was only too pleased to play its part. 'Our guests of honour' were to become the responsibility of the local government board, and a letter was sent to every such board's chairman of each county council including that of Shropshire.

It was hoped there would be many suitable volunteers to take in the refugees, particularly those capable of taking whole families. There were, however, concerns that the refugees may have been seen as cheap labour and great pains were taken to ensure that this did not happen. There was also particular concern that the women and children should be placed in appropriate homes where they would be safe. In addition, all refugees were to be checked by a doctor before being placed.

It wasn't long before the people of Ludlow learned of the plight of the Belgian refugees who were soon to arrive on our shores. Not only were they ready to help those in distress from their town and country and make comforts for the soldiers and sailors on active duty, but now they also turned their attentions to helping those Belgians who had been forced to flee their homes. Talks and plans were in hand to see how many refugees the town could accommodate, where they would live and where the money would come from to keep them.

A lot of fund-raising for this cause was needed and it got off to a good start in September 1914 when a gramophone adorned with the flag of Belgium and the Union Jack was paraded through the streets of Ludlow; the resulting collection was £8.

When it was announced by the government that the whole country was expecting an influx of refugees from Belgium in 1914, it was not long before a committee to organize their accommodation and welfare was set up in Ludlow. With Mayor Mr Valentine at the helm and the grammar school headmaster and a bank manager to help, things soon moved on with a party of fifteen refugees arriving at Ludlow Station.

St Peter's Roman Catholic Church, Ludlow; an important place for the Belgian refugees finding sanctuary in the town. (*Author's own*)

They were treated like royalty, being whisked away to a civic reception from whence they were transported to their temporary accommodation. Those offering such homes were paid around 12s a week per refugee housed by them.

Such houses in Ludlow were at 12 Dinham where, among others, a wine merchant, the proprietor of an import/export business and a lady dressmaker were homed. It was soon discussed how much living allowance each refugee should be awarded. Many donations came in

12 Dinham, where some of the Belgian refugees found a temporary home. (*Author's own*)

from a variety of sources but it was up to the committee of ladies to decide what that amount should be and it wasn't straightforward. Not all the refugees were of equal social standing, therefore some of them who were used to a certain lifestyle expected more than others. They were awarded an extra shilling a week per person. They were also awarded a clothing allowance, which again depended on the social class of the refugee.

The refugees accepted this charity graciously. However, they were keen to find employment to help pay their own way. There was even a Belgian wedding: the Roman Catholic Church saw the joining together of Edmund Verlinden and Julia de Groof who were refugees staying in Ashford Carbonell but had chosen to settle in Birmingham. It was hoped that they would return to Belgium when the war was over and it was safe for them to go home. However, by 1916 many of the refugees had already left the town to return to their homeland. All in all, Ludlow and the surrounding area accommodated eighty-eight Belgian refugees.

**Troops on Leave**
In January 1918 it was noted in the town that troops arriving home on leave were quite often left at Ludlow Station with no means of getting home other than walking, also encumbered with their heavy kit. Because the area was rural in nature, many of them lived a fair few miles out of Ludlow and a call went out to the townspeople to help, as did a request to the local MP Mr Rowland Hunt.

In response, the Ludlow Our Shilling Fund was started. Soldiers and sailors returning home on leave were to be transported by car if they lived more than 3 miles away. Corve Garage in the town would provide this taxi service for a small charge.

By 9 February 1918 the fund had received donations of £42 7s 9d, equal to 847¾ shillings. To date eight soldiers had taken up the offer of transport. By June 1918 the Our Shilling Fund had raised £171 15s 3d and had helped to transport sixty-nine servicemen to their homes. A Flag Day held in June 1918 raised a further £33 18s 2d.

War Weapons Week was held from 17 to 22 June. The aim of this was to raise £15,000 to 'win our gun'. Other towns had fallen short of the total but Ludlow was determined to achieve it. The amount raised in that week totalled £12,000. People were urged to 'fire their money' at the Huns. By the end of June they had exceeded their aim and actually raised almost £22,000.

A grand patriotic fête was also held in June in the castle grounds in aid of the Red Cross, Queen Mary's Needlework Guild, the KSLI PoW fund and the Discharged and Demobilized Soldiers' and Sailors' Fund. There were athletics, horticultural and vegetable shows. This fête raised an amazing £447 17s 8d: quite an achievement considering it was wartime, rationing was in full swing and everyone was war-weary and

A field gun in Ludlow, 1919, that was obtained with the help of Lord Powis when towns and cities across the country could bid for war relics. The gun remained until the Second World War when it was used for scrap metal towards the war effort. (*Courtesy of Shropshire County Museum Service*)

desperate for it to come to an end. The total was divided between the four charities mentioned above.

**War Savings Bonds**
Charities were not the only organizations seeking money; the government was too. In 1914 the gold reserves for Great Britain amounted to around £9 million. Wars are extremely costly, so the government introduced a scheme in which people were encouraged to buy war bonds. These were essentially a loan to the government that would be repaid to the purchaser in the 1920s. They were launched, with various interest rates, in 1914, 1915 and 1917. Once again, it was billed as patriotic to buy them. The government simply couldn't finance the war without them. Shropshire certainly took all this on board, buying bonds worth a respectable £230,810.

In December 1916 the Ludlow Local Central Committee of the National War Savings Committee opened for enquiries in an office at 17 King Street. They also sold War Savings Certificates. A meeting organized by the Ludlow Central War Saving Committee in November 1917 recognized that low wages in the town made it difficult for people to save; nevertheless, every little helped. Up to that date they had 1,148 members who had bought 6,558 certificates between them.

In February 1917 Ludlow embarked on a Victory Loan campaign with a public meeting held in the Town Hall. This was attended by a 'large and enthusiastic' crowd who were encouraged by the council to support the war effort and were told how they could do so. Posters were displayed proclaiming 'Your Money or Their Lives'. It was hoped that people's investment in Victory Loans would help to shorten the war.

The dawn of March 1918 saw War Bonds Boom Week in which Ludlow was to boost war bond purchases to help support the cost of the war. The bureau at 17 King Street, Ludlow was the place to go to buy the bonds. The aim of the week was to raise enough funds to buy six aeroplanes: £15,000.

King Street today, where the War Savings Committee had their offices. (*Author's own*)

**War Pensions**

After the war, those men who had seen active service but did not remain within the armed forces were expected to retrain and undertake some form of occupation, allowing for their wounds and disabilities. The Discharged Soldiers' and Sailors' group voted in favour of their colleagues in Wolverhampton's adoption of a resolution urging that all the political parties should work together to ensure a good pension for soldiers and sailors and that this should be administered correctly and quickly.

In February 1917 the Ludlow branch of the Naval and Military Pensions Committee assembled for its fortnightly meeting to discuss how many sailors from Ludlow had taken part in the Battle of Jutland. Miss Rotton from Stokesay Court Auxiliary Hospital was on this committee, along with the mayor and others. It was discovered that two such sailors had been involved and they would be given a share of a £214 contribution from New Zealand to help them.

The committee heard many cases of hardship brought about by the war, including one involving the wife of a Ludlow soldier whose business was struggling as a result of her customers being called up. The chairman made the remark that 'She is suffering through the war. We are all suffering.' The committee, being sympathetic to her plight, agreed to pay the difference between the 12s 6d she now received and the 30s her husband used to give her, less her husband's keep.

The committee also received regular circulars informing them of any changes regarding pensions and grants. In January 1918 they were told that preferences for paid employment should first be given to discharged soldiers and that they now had the power to award emergency grants in cases where there was child cruelty or the wife was for some reason not entitled to the separation allowance. May 1918 saw the introduction of a new pension scale for soldiers and sailors which saw an increase in their allowances.

**Food Parcels**

It was discussed in January 1918 that food parcels should be sent to British prisoners of war in Germany. There would be three food parcels a fortnight for each prisoner: each parcel would weigh 10 to 11lb when packed and would cost 7s 6d to post. There would be one bread parcel and cigarettes per week. The food parcels contained essential items such as margarine or dripping, meat, tinned fish, soups, tea and milk; a very welcome gift for those men.

### Bedsocks, Eggs and a Patriotic Donkey

Queen Mary herself issued an appeal to the women of the Empire, urging them to supply 300,000 pairs of woollen socks and 300,000 knitted or woven body belts for the 'gallant soldiers' to see them through the winter months.

The Hon. Mrs Lindley, Chairwoman of the Work Committee of the Shropshire Voluntary Aid Organization, reported that between September and October 1914 4,046 articles had been received with 3,994 of these having been despatched. This included 1,058 pairs of socks, 1,000 day shirts and 253 bed-jackets. They were distributed between the Red Cross, the KSLI and St John's Ambulance, with provisions also distributed among the Belgian refugees in local areas.

There was no shortage of willing helpers and lists reproduced in the newspapers advised what was most needed. Some of these items included handkerchiefs, bootlaces, newspapers, chocolate, sweets, peppermints, dried fruit, briar pipes and tobacco pouches, cigarettes and papers, small tins of boracic ointment, borated Vaseline for sore feet, antiseptic powder, pocket knives, postcards, lead pencils, soap, leather soles for boots, toilet paper and thin woollen sleeveless vests. It took a lot to keep a man at the front line and a few home comforts were most definitely welcome. Something familiar and comforting such as chocolate could improve the morale of the soldiers, even in the direst environment.

To help the local hospitals, Ludlow also had a strong volunteer base with a production line making medical supplies. There was a branch of the Red Cross in Ludlow at 5a Old Street which in the first six months of 1916 produced a staggering 11,480 items such as bandages and splints. The local hospitals were first supplied with their products, after which the remainder was despatched to Red Cross depots.

So many fêtes, sales of work, teas and dances took place. You name it, they did it to raise money for the war effort. There was a football match for the Red Cross Society played on Temeside Football Ground in April 1916. The two teams were the Railway Men and Mr C. Harris's XI. Despite some in Ludlow renouncing such entertainment in wartime, there was a large crowd and £5 was raised.

Elsie Jones has received the following post card from a Canadian soldier who was given an egg with her name upon it:

"I expect you will be wondering where one of your eggs has strayed to. Well, I must say it is a long way from home, as it has got as far as the Isolation Hospital, Aldershot. I must say it was very nice and fresh, much different to some we have been getting lately; you know the ones I mean, those that speak for themselves 'Bow-wow.' I must say that it is very good of you to send eggs like that to the soldiers, so I only think it right that soldiers should write and thank you, which I do very sincerely.

CORP. WOOLGER."

Letter of thanks for eggs from a soldier. (*Courtesy of Chris Deaves*)

Letter of thanks for eggs from a soldier. (*Courtesy of Chris Deaves*)

Bagthorpe Military Hospital,
Ward No. II, Nottingham,
29, 8, 15.

Dear Master Alan,

I write in answer to your nice gift you made on behalf of us wounded soldiers. I think of you good little boys quite a lot, especially when you see photos of children handing eggs to go to Hospitals to help to make the soldiers healthy and strong again. I was the soldier who received one of your eggs, therefore I owe you my sincere thanks, I quite enjoyed it for tea a day ago. I am pleased to think that even the boys who are growing perhaps to take our place, if necessary in years to come, are doing their bit in the war. It is a grand thought for us chaps to know that you and every one connected are doing their utmost to make us both well and happy. Now I, although I lost a leg in the war to help the country, I have only done as much as what you are doing for the soldiers. So in closing I will thank you once again and with a hearty voice will also wish you good luck and God bless you. Always remember you are a soldier of God and you will grow up a good strong man.

I remain, yours sincerely,
ARTHUR J. CORNISH.

EGG COLLECTION.—Mrs. Fred James has made a good start and is meeting with a willing response in the village district. On July 19th the number of eggs was 50, and on the 26th, it was 40. The second week's number would have been greater but for the Children's Service to which the children brought 86 eggs. Eggs are getting scarcer, but we must try to keep the numbers up, as probably the number of wounded soldiers and sailors will increase. No one need be afraid that the eggs will be gobbled up by the doctors and nurses.

Egg-collection notice in church magazine. (*Courtesy of Chris Deaves*)

There was also a big push regarding egg-collecting. Eggs, being so nutritious, were good for boosting the soldiers' wellbeing and were often sent abroad as well as to the local VAD hospitals. They were most appreciated by the soldiers, as this letter in the local church magazine attests.

In aid of Queen Mary's Needlecraft Guild, an American Tea was held in the Town Hall. The aim of this was to raise funds for new material to make comforts. Those who attended were asked to bring goods to the value of 6d or more which were then to be sold. This event raised an impressive £56 9s 6d.

In May 1916 all the work sent out from the Ludlow branch of the Red Cross had been examined and found to be 'excellent in material and workmanship'. Up until the end of March 1916 the branch had made, among other things, 5,776 swabs, 524 bandages, 177 knitted wash cloths and 33 pairs of slippers.

Even the local farmers got in on the fund-raising efforts. Despite their workforce being depleted and continually being asked to produce more food, they still managed to raise more than £1,000 at a Red Cross sale. This broke all previous records. The best sale of the day was of a 'well-groomed' donkey called Willie who was dressed in patriotic colours. So popular was Willie that he was paraded in the ring for an hour and half, having been bought and sold seventy-seven times in all and he alone raised £269 19s!

**The YMCA**
Another institution concerning Ludlow was the YMCA and its challenge to the townspeople to raise money for two YMCA huts. These were recreation huts for servicemen and within the first couple of weeks of the declaration of war the YMCA had 250 such huts in England. They were often situated by railway stations where troops were passing through.

Soon there would be similar huts in France and Belgium and all areas of combat; around 2,000 in all. They provided food and refreshments and a place for soldiers to stay. Chaplains also held services there and the huts were used to host visiting relatives of wounded men. The YMCA did further good works, as they also provided the troops with free stationery (15,000,000 pieces per month).

Ludlow was to host a Hut Week to raise money for two huts, and £600 a day would be needed to maintain these.

The South Shropshire Farmers' Union had pledged £600 from their parish sales fund for their hut which was destined for France. The town council wanted to raise £600 and already a little over £302 had been subscribed towards their hut. They managed to raise the total sum and the farmers' hut was built in Arras, France with the Ludlow and District hut erected in Hancourt, France.

However, not everyone agreed with how the money was being raised for Church Army huts. One reader of the *LA* sent a letter expressing his disgust that a whist drive was being planned for such purpose: 'Nothing would be more repugnant to Mr Charlie (Head of the CA) than that a festivity should be held at a moment when we are all plunged in such intense anxiety for the fate of many thousands of young men and when we are awaiting the lists of those killed.' He suggested that instead of holding the whist drive, they should just donate the money instead.

In November 1917 the council was thinking about Christmas presents for soldiers and sailors from Ludlow on active service. They agreed on the idea and £33 11s was pledged for this purpose. There would be an appeal in the town for subscriptions and donations. It was hoped that £150 would be raised via subscriptions. They eventually raised a total of £162 12s 11d and had the names of 506 Ludlow soldiers and sailors, each of whom was sent a 5s postal order for Christmas. [Presumably there would have been costs involved in purchasing the postal orders plus the postage charge of sending them. We can only assume that any residual balance was put towards other good causes of the time.]

If it had not been for the efforts and hard work of all the various charities, the war would have been a great deal worse for everyone. Those taking part in the conflict had their morale boosted every time they received something from home, as did the non-combatants who sewed, donated and raised money in all manner of ways.

# CHAPTER 12

# The Wounded Come Home

It is inevitable that with war comes a multitude of casualties and the Great War was no exception. Men were wounded, some severely, in their thousands. The medical stations based near the battlefields and the hospital ships were soon overwhelmed and British thoughts turned to how the country could help the growing number of casualties.

## VAD

In Shrewsbury a meeting was held to discuss how Shropshire would be able to help the military in this respect. The meeting was well attended by Shropshire residents of substance and influence, and it was agreed that arrangements were to be made via the Voluntary Aid Detachments across the county to assist the country in coping with the influx of wounded and sick soldiers.

Major C.R.B. Wingfield, the then Mayor of Shrewsbury and officer of the 3rd KSLI, was there and he was of the opinion that Shropshire people were only too aware of the gravity of what the world was facing, yet they were more than prepared to do their bit to help. Once again, Ludlow was no exception.

Lord Powis also called a meeting to discuss how such a scheme would be organized, together with how the relief of distress would take place. He had the idea of forming a committee comprising himself, the

High Sheriff, Members of Parliament, chairmen of the Courts Council and Quarter Sessions, mayors of all the borough, chairmen of the Rural and Urban District Councils, representatives of the Friendly Societies, the Victoria Nursing Association, Voluntary Aid Detachment and others to organize the arrangements.

Every town and parish would then have a subcommittee and they would be responsible for finding out the level of need on their patch so that the relief funds and services could be fairly distributed. During the meeting Dr Cureton talked about the association's intentions of having both clearing and stationary hospitals. They were already well versed in improvising the ambulance trains and already had plenty of rest stations. What they needed were more buildings that were adaptable for use as auxiliary hospitals for convalescent men.

Mr Bridgman replied that a small committee had met with the intention of forming a further committee in the county for the Voluntary Aid Detachment and had found to their delight that there were many people coming forward to offer their help. A central committee would be responsible for organizing these offers of help and where they could best be used.

Two of the major organizations involved in the war effort both at home and abroad were the British Red Cross and the Order of St John. They formed the Joint War Committee soon after the conflict began, its main role being to help wounded and sick soldiers and sailors.

The Joint War Committee was responsible for organizing its many volunteers, including professionals, into Voluntary Aid Detachments. These detachments played many different roles throughout the war including supplying machinery and services across the conflict zones and at home.

All the VADs had basic first-aid training, with some of them receiving more in-depth nurse training as well. Apart from their nursing duties, they also made items for the hospitals including swabs, bandages, splints and clothing. There were central workrooms in various towns up and down the country, usually set up by prominent and influential local townswomen who would also donate money to buy materials etc. for the volunteer garment-makers to use.

The War Office needed hospitals to house and care for their convalescent soldiers and sailors and local manor houses and stately homes were the obvious choice. Many owners of such properties were

Nurses outside the Drill Hall, Ludlow during the Great War. (*Courtesy of Shropshire County Museum Service*)

only too glad to turn part of their homes into auxiliary hospitals, thereby doing their bit for the war effort.

Shropshire was certainly unprepared for the scenes at Shrewsbury Railway Station in 1915:

> A special Red Cross train arrived with close upon one hundred wounded British soldiers who are to receive care and comfort at the Royal Shrewsbury Hospital and four local hospitals. The arrival of the wounded was witnessed by a large crowd of residents, who were moved to tears in many cases.

Early on in the war the realization that the existing local hospitals would be overwhelmed with casualties from the war led to discussions about private houses being commandeered by the military and, if they passed inspection and were deemed suitable, would play their part in the war effort. Every house deemed satisfactory was turned into a convalescent home for the sick and wounded. They would be run by a commandant with a local doctor taking responsibility for the care of the inmates, assisted by a team of auxiliary nurses. Nationally, by 1918 around 3,000 such hospitals were up and running.

**Auxiliary Hospitals**

In the Ludlow area there were three auxiliary hospitals that opened during 1915: Overton Lodge, Overmead House and Stokesay Court at nearby Onibury.

Owned by local grocer and former Mayor of Ludlow Gaius Smith, Overmead House was situated just off Livesey Road in the town. It was to have thirty beds with Miss Dorothy Marston as commandant; she had been responsible for setting up the Red Cross VAD in Ludlow. Two local doctors – Dr William Farmer and Dr Malin Gilkes – were Overmead House's medical officers.

The local community was keen to help fund all the auxiliary hospitals in the area. In December 1916 a particularly successful bazaar was held in the Town Hall, at which they sold firewood, flowers, plainwork [plain needlework] and flowers, along with refreshments. The visitors were also treated to a musical programme. The sum of £159 was raised which was destined to help supplement the 2s a day per man that the hospital received from the government.

Smaller, though playing no less an important part in the war effort, was Overton Lodge which was owned by Lieutenant Colonel Edward D. Kennedy. It had just eleven beds, one of them situated in a hut. Sister Fowler was in charge, with the commandant being Colonel E. Cook.

The patients at both Overmead House and Overton Lodge were treated to entertainment. They regularly attended tennis and bowls matches at Linney Pavilion and Whitcliffe Bowling Club with tea served on the green afterwards.

However, things did not always run smoothly and, despite the town being eager to receive and help wounded soldiers, some local residents who lived near Overmead House were not impressed with the noise they claimed the convalescent soldiers made after a night in the pub, as shown by this letter in the local paper:

> The wounded Tommies of Overmead Hospital were greatly surprised to be informed that they were creating a disturbance in the town, as some unkindly civilian complained. It is very hard to think, after having the misfortune to be wounded, that we should be insulted after serving our King and Country as we have done.

Other residents of Ludlow agreed with the Tommies: 'The great majority of Ludlow people appreciate what you have done, so please don't worry if one or two of the Pecksniffian breed do complain.'

Stokesay Court, situated in the beautiful South Shropshire countryside, was owned by Margaret Allcroft and she agreed to allow a portion of her house to be used as a hospital from April 1915. What had started out as a ten-bed hospital soon grew to thirty, with Miss Allcroft as commandant alongside her hard-working matron Miss Lilian Weekes, Sister Alice Williams and medical officer Dr Edward Greene.

Stokesay Court. (*Courtesy of Caroline Magnus*)

Unlike most such hospitals across the country, patients at Stokesay Court each had a room to themselves. When it is considered that many of these lads might not have had such a privilege before and perhaps never even seen the countryside before, this experience, after the horror and discomfort of the battlefields, must have been extraordinary for them.

Many fund-raising events were held throughout the duration of the war, the sums raised augmented by donations received from similar

Royal Artillery PoW whist drive, Stokesay Court. (*Courtesy of Caroline Magnus*)

events organized by others in the town. Often the men from Stokesay Hospital would be invited to attend. One such event was in aid of Queen Mary's Needlework Guild and Overmead Hospital for which the Ludlow Old Girls' Society gave two performances in the Town Hall on Boxing Day 1916.

The men played an unrehearsed role in the entertainment by singing *Mother Mackree* and *Down Home in Tennessee* in the interval. They also whistled *Little Grey Home in the West*. The event raised £12 and not only were the men on the receiving end of charitable donations, they also helped to raise money themselves.

## Letters

The letters received by Margaret Allcroft from past inmates shows the high regard and fondness they felt for her and their time at Stokesay Court. They often referred to her as 'mother'. Today there are around 300 letters in the Stokesay Court archives written by former convalescents and their tone shows how much they appreciated their time there.

In May 1917 J. Clarke wrote asking for a hymn book as he had forgotten to ask Margaret for one before his departure: 'I should so much like to take it with me to France again as it will always remind me of the kindness shown to me at Stokesay Court.'

Another letter, written in 1918, told of how much enjoyment was had from the many recitals and concerts held at Stokesay Court: 'I can picture you sitting at the piano playing for the soldiers … Oh yes I soon got to know the latest songs and grimly proceeded to murder them ...'

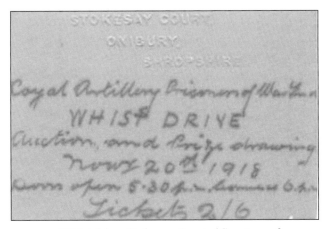

Whist drive, Stokesay Court. (*Courtesy of Caroline Magnus*)

Playing card written on regarding proceeds from a 1918 whist drive. (*Courtesy of Caroline Magnus*)

It is obvious from the letters that the soldiers took part in many games and sports – tennis and fishing to name just a couple – but they also enjoyed winter sports as well:

> I was just thinking about the convalescents. If I was there now I would do double the work what I did before … I was just thinking about the lake as it will be frozen just now and it would be great fun skating on it.
>
> W. Brock, writing from France, 1917.

Some of the letters show that Margaret was more than just a commandant to her 'boys'. They felt they could be very open with her in their letters, telling her their most inner thoughts. The war had had a profound effect upon the men and they often struggled with life out

Stokesay Court: recuperating soldiers and staff, 1918. (*Courtesy of Caroline Magnus*)

As before, year unknown. (*Courtesy of Caroline Magnus*)

of the military, whether it was on leave or upon their discharge, as this letter shows:

> I only wish I was back again to have a few songs and a pleasant evening once more, but the best of friends must part. I must say I hardly know what to put in this letter only kindness because I was happy when I was at Stokesay … I must say that I cannot settled [*sic*] down and I am not at all comfortable over here, but I have got a lot on my mind and I have felt it very much while I have been with the children but they are just getting to know me again. I must close and thanking you for your kindness to me while at that beautiful place called Stokesay Court.
>
> Written by E. Jones

Despite being so busy and devoting her home and her time to the soldiers in her care, Margaret still managed to find love and married Brigadier General Sir John Rotton in 1916. One of her previous patients shared his joy of the news in a letter to her:

The wedding of Sir John Rotton and Margaret Allcroft. (*Courtesy of Caroline Magnus*)

What gave me more pleasure even than getting your letter was to hear of your marriage … It seemed such a waste of a good woman to be living alone in that great big house when you might be making somebody happy.

Written by Arthur G. Hawes in January 1918 from the King George War Hospital, Poona, India.

One of the reasons for Margaret showing such dedication and compassion was the fact that she was no stranger to bereavement and loss herself. Having arrived at Stokesay Court in 1900 following her marriage to its then owner Herbert Allcroft, he died from cancer in 1911. This was followed by the death of two of her brothers in 1914 and 1915. Margaret had not had an easy life and it is a credit to her character and devotion to the cause that she played a great part in the war effort on the home front.

After the war her community-mindedness and sense of duty continued and, among other things, she was elected as Shropshire's first female councillor in 1921. She also became involved with the Girl Guide Movement but died in 1946.

Stokesay Court also provided work for local tradesmen and businesses, as shown by their accounts of December 1917. Bread had been provided by the Craven Arms Co-op Society at £6 12s 9d, with

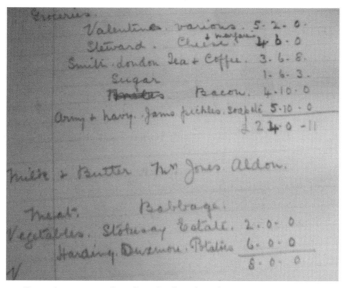

Stokesay Court inventory showing the local tradesmen's names. (*Courtesy of Caroline Magnus*)

Red Cross envelope addressed to Mrs Rotton at Stokesay Court. (*Courtesy of Caroline Magnus*)

various groceries from Valentine's at £5 2s. Expenditure per day for each man was just over 4s 4d.

Stokesay Court was open every Sunday between 2.30pm and 8pm when the public could gain entry and experience one of the Court's teas and talks. The locals brought their own sugar and food. Margaret's aim in this was to entertain the soldiers but also for them to mingle with the visitors and see some new faces.

## Fund-raising

People raised money for the auxiliary hospitals in a number of ways. A cushion competition, for example, raised enough money for 800 cigarettes to be shared between the patients at Overmead and Stokesay Court.

Although the government and the military financed part of the auxiliary hospital services, it was not enough and it was left up to the hospitals themselves and the generosity of the local residents to provide the required additional funds.

Overmead House benefited from £159 raised at a local bazaar held

Recuperating soldiers from Overmead at the Bowling Club, 1916. (*Courtesy of Margory Sheldon*)

Charles Williams' commemorative plaque. (*Courtesy of Stanley Williams*)

in the Town Hall and this was a good example of how local residents supplemented the 2s a day each patient was allocated by the government.

The grounds of the castle in Ludlow were often utilized for such fund-raising in the form of fêtes and sales. Due to the size of the grounds, they could entertain more people there. In 1917 there were approximately 4,000 attendees with 5,000 in the following year. Half of the money raised was earmarked for the Red Cross.

A report on the VAD in Shropshire in April 1915 heralded the good effort the county as a whole was making in tending to wounded and sick soldiers and stated that there had been an impressive 1,544 patients through the various auxiliary hospitals with only six recorded deaths. Since November 1915 7,285 bandages, 22,550 swabs, 959 splints, 310 pressure pads, 50 stretcher cushions, 90 knitted face washers, 16 pneumonia jackets, 274 pairs of slippers, 31 frostbite boots, 40 carbolized shirts, 3 bed tables and 5 jigsaw puzzles had been sent away: a grand total of 31,613 items. The VAD and those in the community helping them clearly meant business.

Sadly in May 1917 Overmead saw its first death of a convalescent soldier: Sergeant Walter C. Sanders of the 16th Canadian Regiment. The families of servicemen who died in the Great War received plaques commemorating the life of their loved one. These were often referred to as 'death pennies'.

## Who Will Care For the Horses?

It wasn't just humans who benefited from the benevolence of local people. In nearby Craven Arms, a Field Veterinary Hospital was set up under the supervision of Lieutenant Colonel Meredith of the Welsh Territorial Division and under the command of Vet Lieutenant Curtis (Shrewsbury). It was designed to receive and treat wounded horses for the duration of the war.

## One Woman's Role

When people think of the Great War they think of men enlisting to fight and the subsequent memorials that are in place up and down the country. If you look at these memorials you would be hard pressed to find any women's names there, but during the war more than 45,000 British women engaged in active service and not all were stationed in VAD hospitals.

Agnes Hadfield was one such woman. Her home life was far from easy, having had an illegitimate child – something of a scandal at the time – and after her marriage failed she became a nurse and served with Queen Alexandria's Imperial Nursing Service in 1914. By 1917, with the war in full swing, Agnes joined the Queen Mary's Army Military Corps.

Some of the duties she performed during the war included driving a team of horses and mules pulling ambulances and supply wagons to the front and ferrying the wounded via motor ambulances when they became available. It was difficult and risky and the women tasked with this job were very courageous indeed.

In fact, Agnes was Mentioned in Dispatches by Field Marshal Sir Douglas Haig. Dispatches were an official report written by a senior officer highlighting courageous or exceptional conduct when faced with the enemy, which was then sent on to high command. She received a certificate signed by Winston Churchill on 16 March 1916.

Despite the risks, Agnes returned home to Hayton's Bent, 4 miles from Ludlow, in 1920 but the war had left its mark on her. Sadly, she went into a mental institution in the early 1920s after suffering recurring nightmares and passed away there in 1942. The war often left its survivors with scars, both physical and mental.

Several members of Agnes's family went into service. Walter Brown, part of the same family, was one of three brothers to fight in

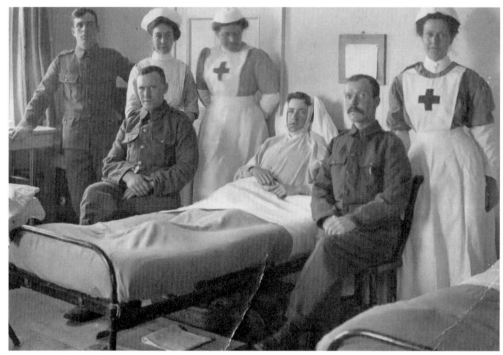

Agnes Hadfield (first nurse on left) on duty in a military ward, possibly during training. (*Courtesy of Clifford Smout*)

Agnes Hadfield also performed the role of one of the pall-bearers at this funeral procession in 1918 (number 11). (*Courtesy of Clifford Smout*)

the Great War. He signed up with the Royal Horse Artillery, served as a gunner with the Royal Field Artillery and died at the age of 19 in 1917.

Fanny, who was Agnes's younger sister, also married a military man by the name of James Gwilt. James survived the war but tragically died in Dovercourt Military Hospital two days after the Armistice was signed.

The Royal Horse Artillery: Walter Brown is holding the crossed knives. (*Courtesy of Clifford Smout*)

James Gwilt and Fanny.
(*Courtesy of Clifford Smout*)

Just as many wounded or sick soldiers were brought back to England to be treated and to recuperate, a lot of treatment was also done on site as shown by this image of a field dentist at work in France in 1915.

Field dentist in France, 1915. (*Courtesy of Wellcome Trust Images*)

RAMC, including local man Tom Wainwright. (*Courtesy of Shropshire County Museum Service*)

By the end of the war 90,000 Red Cross and Order of St John volunteers had helped tend to wounded servicemen and the total amount raised nationally by the Joint War Committee was £21,885,035 with £20,058,355 being spent on hospitals, clothing, grants, medicine and the aftercare of the sick and wounded.

The valuable contribution made by the owners of houses suitable for use as auxiliary hospitals cannot be underestimated. Without them, the military and local hospitals would soon have been inundated and rapidly overwhelmed. It is possible that many more men would have died, had the Red Cross and the Order of St John not been so well-organized.

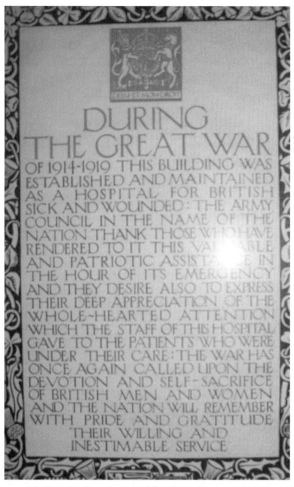

Certificate awarded to Stokesay Court for its role as a VAD hospital during the Great War. (*Courtesy of Caroline Magnus*)

# CHAPTER 13

# The End of the War

*'Let unity do for peace what unity has done for the war.'*

The end of the war couldn't come quickly enough for the people of Ludlow. However, the relief and joy was tinged with a great sense of loss as many of their lives had been changed irrevocably. Even before the Armistice was signed, thoughts were turning to what would happen to the soldiers and sailors returning from the war. It was acknowledged that the country had suffered a severe loss of life, creating a shortfall in labour. Not all the servicemen would stay in the armed forces and part of the plan was to engage them in farming to help in the increased production of home-grown food.

**A World Changed for Ever**
Changes that had taken place at a national level would have a big impact on Ludlow in the years following the war. Millions of people worldwide had been affected by the Great War and a conflict of such ferocity and magnitude was bound to leave a legacy. There were still the poor, the sick and the disabled to be cared for. There were also thousands of women and children left without a husband, father or son and many families did not just suffer the loss of one family member. Often two or more sons had been lost, leaving estates with no heirs to take over. There were also many servicemen still out on the battlefields, yet to be demobilized.

It wasn't only the practicalities and logistics involved that caused

The mayor welcoming the troops back to Ludlow in 1918. (*Courtesy of Shropshire County Museum Services*)

concerns. In 1917 70 per cent of the British GNP (Gross National Product) was spent on the war. The total cost of the Great War from start to finish is estimated at $208 billion. It was going to take some considerable time for the economy to recover and debts to be paid.

Although there was relief that no more lives would be lost on the battlefields, there were a great many men who had been wounded. They would live out the rest of their lives both physically and mentally scarred. For some such men the battle, in many ways, had just begun.

Disabled servicemen who had been medically discharged from the armed forces found themselves back home without the ability to go back to their old jobs and unable to secure new ones because of their disability. They found themselves far from being the war heroes that they were and more of a burden on their local communities and the government. What would the powers that be, who had so urgently and robustly campaigned to get the men to enlist and start fighting, do to help those men who had survived but could no longer care for their families or themselves financially or practically?

The end of the war was a paradox of emotions and situations. On the one hand it was good that the conflict was over but on the other, for all the problems solved by the war, its ending created others. The world was in a state of economic crisis, unemployment was high and resources were scarce, the latter causing prices to escalate. There had been some hard winters during the war, followed by wet springs and summers that affected the harvest. It would be quite some time before life was to become any easier.

**Fighting a New Enemy**

Just as the end of the war appeared to be in sight, a pandemic of the so-called Spanish flu was unleashed and lasted from January 1918 to December 1920. This unusually deadly strain of the virus was so named not because it originated in Spain, but because wartime censorship banned reports of it for fear of lowering morale. However, freedom of the press in neutral Spain allowed it to become public knowledge, giving a misleading impression of its source. The virus became a global catastrophe with a worldwide estimated death toll of some 30 to 40 million and the estimated number of dead in Britain alone was 228,000. It actually caused more fatalities in total than the Great War.

It was thought that men returning from the trenches of France who had been suffering from symptoms of 'La Grippe' brought the virus back from the crowded and insanitary living conditions. It spread very quickly and was highly contagious. Someone who was fit and well in the morning and displaying no symptoms could be dead by the evening, so fast was its progress. Unlike many types of flu which are most dangerous to the very young and the elderly, Spanish flu was particularly potent in those aged 20 to 40 so the young soldiers who had survived the war but were injured or already sick did not stand a chance.

Children across the country could be heard singing a new nursery rhyme:

> I had a little bird
> Its name was Enza
> I opened the window
> And in-flu-Enza

The already depleted national resources and finances couldn't cope with this epidemic. War, lack of good-quality food, rationing, poor health care and a lack of advancement in medicine meant that people's immune systems were not robust and they succumbed more easily to this dreadful illness than they might otherwise have done.

In an attempt to inhibit the spread of the virus, many public buildings were closed for months including churches, halls and picture houses. People were given advice on how to try to prevent themselves catching it, such as daily washing of the nasal passages, avoidance of wearing mufflers, making themselves sneeze several times a day and walking home from work in the fresh air rather than using public transport. The influenza 'scourge', as it was described in the *LA*, spread throughout the town in early November 1918 but residents were told not to be alarmed as all the cases so far had been relatively mild.

Another problem affecting the country was that of sexually transmitted diseases or VD (venereal disease). Generally in peacetime there would be around 300,000 new cases of diseases such as syphilis and gonorrhoea per year, but in the period following the war the numbers increased somewhat. Left untreated, such diseases could cause blindness, insanity and paralysis and they didn't just affect adults as stillbirths and miscarriages were also a potential risk.

There was a great stigma surrounding such diseases as they were regarded by many as punishment for immoral behaviour. However, this was often not the case and great pains were taken by the authorities to dispel this myth. To them, knowledge was power and more people were likely to come forward with symptoms if they were made aware of the consequences of not doing so and weren't too ashamed or embarrassed to seek medical help.

**Positive Thinking**
However, not everything was negative. The Great War had given rise to new innovations and new ideas from the government and policy-makers that would have a long-standing effect on the country for the better. New pension laws, for instance, were introduced to ease the financial difficulties of servicemen who had been disabled during the war and also those who retired from work. In addition, new farming and agricultural methods and research born during the war stayed with the country and developed exponentially.

Medical advances in the treatment of wounds of servicemen from the trenches had a lasting effect on the health of the nation following the war years. This was especially so in terms of innovations in artificial limbs for amputees and plastic surgery for the many men who had returned with facial or other disfigurements.

**Sanctions**
Politically, the government was already working with the allies to impose sanctions on the enemy, with treaties being signed in an attempt to ensure that peace remained and that this war would be 'the war to end all wars'. The world had taken a battering and no one was keen to see it happen again. Britain was certainly at breaking-point and peace was all-important for her recovery.

As ever, the *LA* was there to keep the locals informed of developments and what was happening in the post-war days, weeks and months. In the 16 November 1918 edition of the paper it was reported that Austria-Hungary had surrendered and that the Italian commander-in-chief had signed an armistice. They also printed a notice informing their readers that due to the Armistice there would be no further recruitment into the armed forces and all call-ups yet to be enforced had been cancelled.

The whole world breathed a sigh of relief when, at last, after four arduous years the war finally came to an end. On 9 November 1918 in a railway carriage in a Compiègne forest in France, representatives from Germany, France, Britain and America met to thrash out the terms of an armistice. By 11 November 1918 it was all agreed and was signed at 5am. The fighting was to stop at 11am that very day.

However, it was not until January 1919 that the final details were sorted out in Paris at the Palace of Versailles. Every country sent delegates to stake their claims and state their cases. The Treaty of Versailles was eventually signed in June 1919, with most countries licking their wounds and getting less than they had originally demanded.

Countries that had invaded their neighbouring nations were made to pay for the damage, a debt that would take many years to pay off. Germany was ordered to pay £24 billion and was restricted to an army of no more than 100,000 men. She was banned from owning or building submarines, restricted to six battleships at most and prohibited from having an air force.

The cost to the country both economically and emotionally was huge, as it was for all those involved. This was hardly a mere spat from which everyone could just dust themselves down and carry on as though little or nothing had happened. It would take decades for those involved to get back on their feet and the face of Europe was changed forever.

**Relief**

News of the Armistice reached the local Post Office at 11am on Monday. This led to the townspeople crowding into the centre of town – already busy as it was auction day – where they met with buildings decorated with flags and the celebratory peal of the 'joy bells' from the parish church ringing in their ears.

There were reports of scenes of enthusiastic flag-waving with the young people of the town behaving in a particularly 'boisterous' manner. It was hoped that the young would never again witness such scenes in their lifetimes. Another such war would have seemed inconceivable at the time.

As a result of the jubilant news, the elementary schools were closed with the secondary schools also granted a holiday. Even the grammar school, which had seen many of its old boys go off to war, was involved in the celebrations, albeit with a tone of sadness and respect for those who had not come home. The flagpole in the school grounds was the focal point around which they gathered for their thanksgiving and relief. The Union Jack was raised and saluted and the headmaster Mr Threlfall gave a speech. The National Anthem was sung, as it would be many times over as the celebrations in the town continued.

The Union Workhouse was alerted to the fact that something momentous was happening by their being able to hear the church bells. J.V. Wheeler, Chairman of the Board of Guardians, commented that he was certain they were 'never more glad to hear the church bells'.

As the day went on, the town council held a special meeting at which it was agreed that the town should have a holiday on the following day. In the evening the crowds gathered in the Castle Square where a special exhibition had been set up. They were shown films from various areas where the war had been fought; these were organized by the National War Committee.

The mayor also spoke to the crowds. Included in his address was a reminder that although the war was over, the people of Ludlow still had a duty to those who had taken part in the conflict and to their families. There then followed a service at the parish church at 7.30pm. The poignant hymn chosen to start the service was *All People That on Earth do Dwell* and Psalm 46 was also sung, its theme being about God providing refuge and strength. Prayers of thanksgiving followed, again the National Anthem was sung and the *Hallelujah Chorus* played. The next day had been declared a holiday and a local band organized by Sergeant Major Hogan marched all over the town playing patriotic tunes.

**Life Goes On**
Life immediately following the war was not easy. Mothers who had lost sons, wives who had lost husbands, children who had lost fathers and sisters who had lost brothers would see ex-servicemen walking the streets of Ludlow and wonder why they had survived and their own family members had not. It cannot have been easy for the ex-servicemen either as they tried to come to terms with the loss of their own family members, friends and work colleagues and settle back into civilian life.

**Peace Day**
It was almost a year later on Saturday, 19 July 1919 that the whole country held Peace Day celebrations. Peace Day was a national initiative. It was at first envisaged that it would be a four-day celebration but was later reduced to one day. Not everyone considered it appropriate and thought that the money and effort would be put to better use in building up resources and facilities to help servicemen who had returned and had problems with unemployment and injuries, both mental and physical.

   Although the war was now all but over, the local authorities were still keen to provide for those men and women who had helped with the war effort by encouraging people to donate money to the King's Fund for the Disabled. It was now time for the people of Ludlow to 'show your gratitude and appreciation' to the men who had fought, as a 'practical expression of your gratitude'.

   The end of the Great War hardly meant an end for the need of a steady cash flow. War Savings Bonds turned into peacetime saving and people were urged to continue buying War Savings Certificates because

The Ludlow Peace Tree being planted in 1919. (*Courtesy of Margory Sheldon*)

the country still had 7,000,000 men needing clothes, food and demobilization. In addition, the hospitals were still full of wounded and sick servicemen.

The cost of the war, the repayment of government borrowing and the rebuilding that took place in the years following the end of the conflict took a huge toll on all those countries involved. The part played by local communities was tremendous and the recovery would not have been so rapid without their help. Patriotism and doing one's duty did not dissipate with the sound of the last guns fired in anger. Thoughts now also turned to providing more permanent memorials to the war dead.

# CHAPTER 14

# War Memorials

*'We will remember them.'*

Great Britain lost approximately 743,000 military personnel but in all over 8 million soldiers died during the conflict: a tragedy for all concerned, not less the grieving relatives who frequently had lost their only sons or perhaps several members of the same family. The true figures will never come to light; such is the destructive nature of warfare. Many bodies were never found or identified. This 'lost generation' could never be replaced in the eyes of those who mourned them. Bereaved families were often told that their son or husband had died in the glory of battle, doing his duty for king and country, but that would have been little consolation to them.

There was a great need to prevent anything like this from ever happening again. In an attempt to do this the League of Nations was formed. All member countries were urged to seek to avoid future conflicts and instead of using force as in war, they pledged to try to resolve their differences through discussion, negotiation and compromise.

As is usual in human nature, the best of intentions soon gave way to more disagreements and the war that had been regarded as the war to end all wars proved not to be the case. The Second World War was just twenty years away and yet more names would be added to the thousands of war memorials that had popped up around Britain and abroad. Many fathers who had fought in the Great War could only stand back and watch with a dreadful sense of déjà vu as their sons packed up their troubles in their old kit bags and smiled their way off to war. Marshal Foch was right when he said that it wasn't peace, merely a twenty-year armistice.

**Remembrance**

The people of Ludlow had been attending church and memorial services throughout the war but as early as March 1916 in the editorial of the parish magazine thoughts and discussions turned to how the war dead might best be remembered, what kind of memorial would be most appropriate and where it should be situated. The obvious place was in churches or churchyards but there were concerns that the design would have to be sympathetic to the surroundings and not an eyesore: 'What has to be said should be said gravely, simply and quietly.'

For Ludlow, the Roll of Honour is situated inside the front porch of St Laurence's Church. On the wall there is a memorial with the names of 138 men who were killed during the Great War. The heaviest year for deaths was 1918 with fifty-eight local men killed and not all of them had died in battle.

Picture of part of the Roll of Honour inside St Laurence's Church, Ludlow. (*Author's own*)

The more modern war memorial in the centre of Ludlow. Note there are currently no names on it: the town has commissioned an engraver to add them this year. (*Author's own*)

Things were not, however, straightforward. There was heated debate between the churches as to where the memorial should be situated and what form it should take. They formed a committee for this purpose but it was disbanded when a consensus could not be reached. A further committee was appointed which decided to have some memorial boards in the Town Hall; this is why there were two sets of wooden memorial boards. There is also another modern war memorial in the town centre that was added at a much later date.

National memorials were also built, such as The Cenotaph in London and the Grave of the Unknown Soldier in Westminster Abbey, and those who fell abroad are buried in numerous memorial cemeteries such as those at Thiepval and Ypres. Many towns and villages across the country wanted to remember and honour their war dead, their local lads, their sons, brothers, fathers and lovers in their own way.

Many cities, towns and villages in Great Britain had honoured the war dead who had enlisted for duty earlier on in the war by having rolls of honour made up, many of which were published in the local newspapers. In Ludlow they also had war shrines comprising lists of soldiers at the front; these were attached to the walls

A sign at Ludlow Cemetery showing that some of Ludlow's war dead are buried there. (*Author's own*)

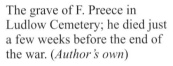

The grave of F. Preece in Ludlow Cemetery; he died just a few weeks before the end of the war. (*Author's own*)

of houses and in the streets of the town, particularly Mill Street and Raven Lane.

It was the Civic Arts Association that commenced important educational work about memorials. The thinking of the time was that memorials should not be fleeting: they are a lasting monument to the fallen who gave their lives in their millions. It was important that each memorial should speak of the country's loss, both in the words chosen to adorn the memorial and the style of the memorial itself.

Unfortunately some memorials are incomplete or incorrect as at the time they were erected many families, whose responsibility it was to inform the authorities of their loved one's or family member's name – someone who was missing, presumed dead – simply refused to do so. While they were missing, even months or years later there was still hope. To etch their loved one's name in stone next to the fallen from their town or village would have felt like giving up on them and admitting that they were very probably dead.

Not all memorials were situated in churchyards. Some adorn village squares or town centres, while others are in schools, village halls and workplaces. Possibly it is the memorials within the walls of schools that are the most thought-provoking, as only a couple of years before finding themselves on the battlefields and giving their lives for king and country, these fine young men had been sitting behind desks, keen to learn and full of potential. Their dreams were cut short and never to be realized. Ludlow Grammar School in particular had provided a fertile breeding ground for officer material.

**Poppies**

Memorials were being planned, designed and erected all over Britain, as well as on many sites of or near the battlefields in France and Belgium and also further afield. However, as the first anniversary of the end of the war drew near in November 1919, thoughts turned to a more formal national day of remembrance with a three-minute silence for those who had sacrificed their lives.

It wasn't long before the public took this to their hearts and the Flanders poppy became the emblem for those who had died, serving as a poignant symbol of remembrance and peace. The poppy was an American idea that was adopted by the Royal British Legion and the inspiration came from the millions of poppies that grew in the churned-

Ludlow Town Civic Service of Remembrance, Sunday, 3 August 2014. (*Author's own*)

up, shelled battlefields of Flanders, Belgium; the only sign of life amid the devastation and the only flower to be seen growing in a sea of mud and human remains.

Even today, at the time of writing this book, a special exhibition was held at the Tower of London depicting a sea of ceramic poppies, one for each serviceman that lost his life. The display was a remarkable one, eventually covering an area equivalent to sixteen football pitches.

Special services are still held, wreaths laid and poppies worn to remember the war dead on Remembrance Day each year. Funds raised from the Royal British Legion's poppy sales are used to support both those currently serving in the armed forces and military veterans from earlier conflicts.

## The Next Generation

At nearby Ludford in 2014 they held a ceremony and family day to celebrate the unveiling of a new memorial so that their war dead who died in battle 100 years ago could be honoured.

Some of the descendants of those from Ludford who had sacrificed their lives in the Great War attended a moving ceremony. Even though

The unveiling of the Ludford War Memorial, 2014. (*Author's own*)

The residents and some families unveiling the Ludford War Memorial. (*Author's own*)

IN REMEMBRANCE OF
THE MEN OF LUDFORD PARISH
WHO SERVED THEIR COUNTRY DURING WWI 1914 - 1918

| | | | |
|---|---|---|---|
| E. ANTHONY | A. E. GALLEY | E. J. PRICE | T. WARD |
| S. E. BERRY | W. J. GRIFFITHS | E. S. PRICE | W. A. WARDMAN |
| T. H. BEVAN | W. E. JACKSON | H. T. PRICE | H. T. WEAVER |
| A. BLOOM | W. B. MASON | H. PRITCHARD | J. A. WEAVER |
| H. BRADLEY | H. C. MEREDITH | W. J. SANDERS | A. C. WILLIAMS |
| G. H. BROWN | J. NORTHWOOD | A. SAUNDERS | A. V. WILLIAMS |
| J. CHARMER | A. J. O'CONNOR | G. SAUNDERS | H. G. WILLIAMS |
| G. W. CHILDES | F. PENNY snr | G. W. SAUNDERS | H. WILLIAMS |
| G. G. W. DAY | F. PENNY jnr | H. SAUNDERS | R. C. WILLIAMS |
| R. E. DAY | H. F. PENNY | P. H. SAUNDERS | T. WILLIAMS |
| T. DEAN | R. J. PENNY | E. T. SMITH | A. WYLDE |
| F. EVANS | T. PERRY jnr | H. THOMAS | |
| C. EVASON | G. H. POUND | R. V. TWIDDY | |
| B. G. FARMER | F. PREECE | H. W. WARBURTON | |

Ludford War Memorial. (*Author's own*)

the conflict took place so long ago, the sons, husbands, brothers, uncles and others are still remembered today.

Ludlow was not without its own taste of fame during the war years. One of the most famous poets of his day was Alfred Edward Housman (1859–1936), who wrote the poem *The Recruit* and the collection of poetry entitled *A Shropshire Lad*. These well-known works were notable for their pessimism and preoccupation with death, without the benefit of religious comfort (Housman himself was an atheist), and during the war years they struck a resounding chord with their readers. However, after the war he wrote a number of works to commemorate the war dead, including *Epitaph on an Army of Mercenaries* to honour the BEF which was originally a small body of professional soldiers.

*The Recruit* speaks of young men leaving their homes and everything they have known to go to war and to come back a hero

'While Ludlow Tower Shall Stand'. It mentions the bells calling and the bustling market of Ludlow and how the recruit should 'Make the hearts of comrades be heavy where you die.'

Although Housman never lived in Shropshire he was taken with its wide open spaces and the Shropshire hills. He was born a few miles away from Shropshire in a small hamlet on the outskirts of Bromsgrove, Worcester and settled in London in his later years. There is a memorial to him situated at St Laurence's Church.

The Great War was a time of tragedy and sacrifice, but it was also a time of transition and a wake-up call that alerted Great Britain to the need for a bigger and more efficient army. It was also a wake-up call to the world: a war of such

A.E. Housman's memorial situated on the outer wall of St Laurence's Church, Ludlow. (*Author's own*)

magnitude and ferocity with the loss of so many young lives and the maiming and disabling of many others could not be allowed to happen again. War memorials are a symbol of loss but they are also a bringer of hope. If the names of those who died are carved into stone, metal or wood, we will remember them.

Unfortunately for the people of Ludlow and their fellow countrymen, the Armistice proved to be but a mere twenty-year break until the Second World War broke out in 1939 and the all-too-familiar scenes of young men marching off to war, many not to return, were played out once again. Despite the hopes of all concerned, the Great War would not be the last time that the people of Ludlow would be called upon to show their courage and strength.

# Index